JOSÉ MARTÍ

Epic Chronicler of the United States in the Eighties

José Martí

EPIC CHRONICLER OF THE UNITED STATES IN THE EIGHTIES

BY

MANUEL PEDRO GONZÁLEZ

With an Introduction by
Sturgis E. Leavitt

Chapel Hill
THE UNIVERSITY
of North Carolina
PRESS

Copyright, 1953, by

THE UNIVERSITY OF NORTH CAROLINA PRESS

MANUFACTURED IN THE UNITED STATES OF AMERICA

VAN REES PRESS • NEW YORK

INTRODUCTION

Latin Americans have never been as addicted to travel as have North Americans, but many of them have visited the United States and have taken the trouble to write down their impressions. Indeed, a fairly extensive library could be assembled, if all the books written by Latin Americans about the United States were to be collected in one place.

Curiously enough, the most popular of these studies of the United States, and the one that has exercised the most influence upon the thinking of Latin America, was written by a man who never visited the United States. This was *Ariel,* written in 1900 by José Enrique Rodó, a Uruguayan, famous then, and famous now for his masterful style. Rodó is one of the two most gifted essayists of Spanish America.

In a clarion call to the youth of Spanish America, Rodó urges young men to be appreciative of beauty in all its forms, and to cultivate a life of the spirit with high ideals and lofty aspirations. The great danger to this mode of life, so Rodó believed, was utilitarianism, represented so fully by the United States.

Rodó recognizes much that is good in the United States: its respect for authority, its demonstration of the power of hard work, its spirit of cooperation, its insatiable curiosity, its interest in education, its admirable efficiency, its energy, its optimism.

With all this, however, the North American has never attained good taste. Furthermore, education in the United States is principally for the masses and results in a general level of mediocrity. There is no place in United States' education for the superior spirit. The morality of the North Americans is a practical one, "la moral de Franklin." Material prosperity is the great ideal of the country. North Americans are not merely satisfied with their special kind of civilization, but they want to impose it upon others. "They would aspire to rewriting Genesis and getting themselves on the front page."

Among the Spanish Americans who wrote about the United States before Rodó, three stand out because of the prominence they attained in their own day and the respect they still enjoy. These three were José María Heredia, inspired lyric poet of Cuba; Domingo Faustino Sarmiento, educator, statesman, and president of Argentina; and José Martí, the great Cuban patriot.

José Mariá Heredia left his native Cuba and came to Boston in December, 1823. He suffered terribly from the cold. His ink almost froze in his pen, so he tells us. Among the things that he had not seen in his native land and upon which he comments were the absence of beggars, the large horses, and the nameplates on all the houses.

The most important visit that Heredia made was to Niagara Falls. This trip was notable not only on account of the bad manners of the people in the stagecoach and on the Erie Canal, but for the fact that Heredia wrote an "Ode to Niagara," destined to become famous throughout the Spanish-speaking world. Heredia was one of the first and one of the most effective publicity agents for Niagara Falls that this country has known. Practically every Spanish American who has read anything, has read Heredia's "Oda a Niágara," and is moved thereby to visit this great natural spectacle.

Domingo Faustino Sarmiento came to the United States on an educational errand—to talk with Horace Mann about a report that Mann had written on education in Europe. This visit to Horace Mann took place in August, 1847. After the interview, Sarmiento made an extensive tour of the United States and even went as far north as Canada.

Sarmiento has no little to say about the bad manners of United States citizens. He relates, for example, how he saw a number of young men in one of the best hotels and was shocked to observe that not one of them could sit properly in a chair. Two had their feet on the table, one rested his feet on the cushion of a nearby chair, another had his leg over the arm of the chair, another had his legs drawn up on the cushion, another had his legs around the back of his chair. Other habits that attracted the attention of Sarmiento were the ever-present chewing tobacco, snatching a cigar out of one person's (Sarmiento's) mouth in order to light the American's cigar, reading over one's shoulder, and pushing roughly through doors. The Yankees, so Sarmiento writes, are the rudest "animalitos with clothes on" in the world.

Notwithstanding the bad manners of the North Americans, Sarmiento had the greatest of admiration for their energy and inventiveness, for the material comfort they enjoyed, their fine hotels, luxurious river boats, the freedom given women, and the way they went on long trips without giving the matter any particular concern.

Sarmiento writes with enthusiasm about the spirit of cooperation which he saw everywhere in this country, the political consciousness of the people, their interest in education, their spirit of independence, their devotion to hard work, and their confidence in themselves. Sarmiento had no hesitation in predicting a great future for the United States.

Unlike Heredia and Sarmiento, Martí spent many years in the United States, and, also unlike them, he learned English, even though it cost him great efforts. His was no casual acquaintance with this country. He came to know it intimately and he wrote, not travel impressions, but long articles about the important events of the day: holidays, political events, art expositions, strikes, the Brooklyn bridge, the death of great men, etc., etc. These articles were published in the principal newspapers of Spanish America, principally in *La Nación* of Buenos Aires, from 1882 to 1891. Written, as they were, in admirable Spanish, they made the United States known as it was never known before; better known, indeed, than it has ever been since. Martí was a good observer, he had a keen interest in men and events, and he had a command of Spanish second to none in his time.

Manuel Pedro González here analyzes Martí's contributions to the understanding of the United States in Latin America. Some historians may not agree with González' interpretation of political happenings, but his comments are interesting, stimulating, and instructive. He has made a sincere effort to present Martí in the United States, and to show the stand he took toward what happened there in one of the most significant periods of its history.

But more important than the picture of life in the United States is Martí himself. González presents to the North American public for the first time the figure of the great Cuban patriot and martyr. Although González does not have space to develop the full stature of the Cuban thinker and man of action, he does present Martí at one of the most crucial periods of his life, and he gives us an insight into the genius of one of the greatest figures in the history of America.

STURGIS E. LEAVITT

Kenan Professor of Spanish, University of North Carolina

PREFACE

A great writer is a perpetual guide and counselor. If, in addition to his intellectual loftiness, he is a great man, such a writer becomes a permanent source of inspiration and a comforting and stimulating friend. This is particularly true in tragic times like the present. We should read and cogitate on the teachings of such "eternal companions" in these days of exacerbated nationalism and super-patriots, of frenzied hysteria on the one hand, and cynical conformism and submissiveness on the other, of irrational fear and distrust everywhere. In the agony of the present impasse which mankind seems to have reached, we should seek guidance from the mental and moral beacons of the past. One such beacon is José Martí.

In the nineteenth century, democracy produced in the Western Hemisphere a group of truly great leaders and thinkers. There were faith and vitality in Democratic ideals. In the United States the creed of democracy bred men of the caliber of Thomas Jefferson, Abraham Lincoln, Horace Greeley, Ralph Waldo Emerson, Henry David Thoreau, Wendell Phillips, Peter Cooper, Henry George, Brooks Adams, and many others whose peers are lamentably lacking today. The same was true of nineteenth-century Latin America, and again a corresponding scarcity of high-caliber men is easily discernible there at present.

The most prominent and indefatigable apostle of freedom and liberty Latin America has produced is José Martí. Not only was he concerned with relations between the individual and the ruling class, or the individual and the state, but also with the principles that should govern the relations between countries. Hence, the timeliness—and universality—of his creed. He never systematized his ideas on this subject—or regarding any other matter—nor did he gather them in book form. (Martí never had the time, nor the peace of mind necessary to write books. He was more interested in disseminating ideas than in writing treatises.) As in the cases of Emerson, Thoreau, Phillips, Cooper, and Brooks Adams, the ideas of Martí about human relations, whether in the social or the international panorama, are grounded in ethical principles of social and economic justice, of equality and respect for all. The dignity of the human being is the cornerstone of his social philosophy, and in defense of this ideal he fought all his life and for it he finally died.

In these times of war psychosis, of reciprocal animosity, of fear and distrust between East and West, it is comforting to read the writings of men like José Martí, who considered himself a brother of every human being. He knew that at the bottom of all wars and international conflicts, there have always been economic interests. The present struggle between the two giants of the planet implies also a class conflict. Martí foresaw—and predicted—the class strife which, in his judgment, could be avoided only by a new and fairer concept—and distribution—of wealth, by an economic leveling-off policy that would eliminate the hideous contrasts between multimillionaires on the one hand and destitute working masses on the other.

Because everything he wrote was inspired by deep sympathy and tenderness, coupled with a boundless love of humanity; because in the apostolic crusade that was his life, he proved himself to be always pure, disinterested, and wise, Martí has become one of the most beloved heroes of Latin America. In the United States, on the other hand, he is practically unknown despite the fact that he interpreted and spread abroad its culture and extolled the merits and virtues of its great men and institutions. In January, 1953, the Hispanic world will commemorate the first centennial of his birth. The present study purports to be an anticipation of and a contribution to that celebration. The author hopes that eventually the people of the United States will become acquainted with Martí and will recognize him for what he is: one of the most admirable men mankind has produced. In a certain way he belongs to the United States also because he lived in this country for fifteen years and contributed toward enriching and disseminating its culture. Unfortunately, practically nothing of what Martí wrote is available in English translation. It is to be hoped that on the occasion of his centennial commemoration, this deficiency will be remedied. The ideas and ideals of great men, as well as the inspiring example of their lives, constitute the priceless inheritance of humanity. Such treasures do not belong to any particular people or country, but to mankind, and should be available in every language. A volume or two of selections from Martí, if adequately translated, would be a very valuable addition to American literature. Even more important and enriching perhaps would be the translation of a collection of his apothegms in which he coined, so to speak, his philosophy of life and condensed his political and social ideas. Of such maxims, the German writer, Emil Ludwig, said, "Hundreds of aphorisms in such a vigorous and penetrating style that they could have been written by Nietzsche, have been gathered in a magnificent collection of his works. If they were translated, these aphorisms would be sufficient to convert Martí into the spiritual guide of the world at the present moment."

MANUEL PEDRO GONZÁLEZ

University of California at Los Angeles
August, 1952

CONTENTS

	PAGE
Introduction, by Sturgis E. Leavitt	v
Preface	ix
Historical Perspective	1
Life of a Hero	5
Man of Culture and Ideals	14
Man of Destiny	18
The United States in the Eighties	22
Martí, Chronicler of Transformation	25
A Plutarchian Portrayer	31
Interpreter of the Social Panorama	46
David and Goliath	56
Notes	73

JOSÉ MARTÍ

Epic Chronicler of the United States in the Eighties

Historical Perspective

THE YEAR 1900 marked a turning point in the prolific Spanish American bibliography regarding the United States. Up to that date, we may safely say that Spanish American commentators on the life, institutions, and customs of this country were generally friendly, and frequently laudatory. Not even the dismemberment of Mexico in 1847, so deeply resented by Spanish America at the time, hindered seriously the favorable disposition of the Latin American writers towards the United States during the last forty years of the nineteenth century. Occasionally there were references and even angry protests against the agitation of some of the superpatriots of the United States who clamored for annexation of new territories or demanded that the national boundaries be extended to the Isthmus of Tehuantepec, or even to that of Panama; but since these expressions of imperialist designs had not crystallized into a policy, but were rather sporadic outbursts, usually limited to professional politicians, no alarm was felt.

The first official manifestation of the arrogant spirit of imperialism took place in 1895. It had been gathering momentum for over a decade but so far had found expression only in some journals and in the speeches of certain Republican leaders. This time, however, the culprit was not an expansionist publication or a Republican senator, but none other than President Grover Cleveland himself through his Secretary of State, Richard Olney, whose statement, known as the Richard Olney pronouncement, was motivated by a dispute between England and Venezuela over the boundary separating the latter from British Guiana. In the words of Harold Underwood Faulkner, this document is "a note that for its truculence and swaggering tone is probably without parallel in diplomatic history." [1]

The imperialistic expansion of the United States was now accelerated. In 1898 Hawaii and Guam were annexed, and part of the Samoa Islands in 1899. In 1898 the United States drove Spain from all her possessions in the Caribbean and in the Pacific and occupied Cuba, Puerto Rico, and the Philippines. In 1902 it imposed the Platt Amendment upon Cuba and took over Guantánamo Bay. The unsavory Panama affair took place the following year. The series of armed interventions and arbitrary acts perpetrated by the U. S. Navy and the Marines in practically all the countries bordering the Caribbean during the next two decades is too long to recount here. During the period 1898-1903, the phrase "manifest destiny" became a threat for Latin America. These events really frightened Spanish American statesmen and writers, dispelled their naive conception of the Monroe Doctrine, and weakened their trust in their neighbor to the north.

In a recent history of United States diplomacy in the twentieth century, George F. Kennan has described the lust for expansion and power at the turn of the century in the following words:

"Similarly, when one notes the variety of arguments put up by the expansionists for the territorial acquisitions of 1898, one has the impression that none of them was the real one—that at the bottom of it all lay something deeper, something less easy to express, probably the fact that the American people of that day, or at least many of their more influential spokesmen, simply liked the smell of empire and felt an urge to range themselves among the colonial powers of the time, to see our flag flying on distant tropical isles, to feel the thrill of foreign adventure and authority, to bask in the sunshine of recognition as one of the great imperial powers of the world." [2]

Justified by this behaviour, the best writers of Spanish America concluded that the real danger to the independence and sovereignty of their respective countries did not lie in the East, as in bygone days, but in the North, and a cataract of *anti-Yanqui* literature began to flow from the printing presses of the Latin American countries. It subsided during the years 1933-1945—the Good Neighbor policy period—but is reappearing again. The first broadside of this literary offensive against the United States was fired in 1900 by the most outstanding essayist of the present century in Spanish America, José Enrique Rodó, in his now famous book *Ariel*. This antagonistic and frequently biased literary product of the twentieth century, which United States meddlings in the Caribbean and elsewhere provoked, has inevitably increased the nationalistic spirit of the masses in the Spanish-speaking countries of the Americas. At the same time, it has fostered a distrustful attitude toward the United States that did not exist in the previous century.

The foregoing historical statement should suffice to place José Martí in adequate perspective. Very little is known in the United States about this extraordinary writer and even more extraordinary man. My purpose here is to examine that period of his life during which he resided in New York and that aspect of his intellectual activity in which he revealed himself as one of the keenest and most profound observers and interpreters of the life, institutions, and men of the United States. Probably few North Americans realize that this frail little man of genius frustrated—twice in a decade—the plans and desires of the United States government and finally helped to deprive it of a coveted territory whose possession it had sought during the whole nineteenth century.

Up to the present, none of his magnificent essays on American life, public men, and great literary figures has been translated into English. Equally regrettable is the fact that nobody in the United States has ever written a biography of Martí or a critical analysis of his writings and interpretation of that country.[3]

Given the scant information that most people have about him, perhaps a brief biographical sketch of Martí may not be out of place before discussing his role in relation to the United States.

Life of a Hero

JOSÉ MARTÍ was born in Havana, Cuba, on January 28, 1853, of Spanish parentage. His family was always poor and before he was fifteen he had to work as an assistant bookkeeper to help in the support of his home. Thanks to the generosity of a distinguished Cuban poet and educator, Rafael María de Mendive, who early discovered the boy's talent and sterling character, Martí was able to finish grammar school and begin his secondary education. He was not yet through high school when he published several poems advocating freedom and independence for Cuba. Because of his patriotic zeal and activities, he was jailed by the tyrannical Spanish government of the island and, when he was only seventeen, was finally condemned to six years at hard labor. After serving part of the sentence, the penalty was commuted to that of exile to Spain.

In Spain Martí suffered great hardships. In addition to his extreme poverty, his health failed because of the physical injuries he had received in jail. He succeeded, nevertheless, in completing his academic training at the universities of Madrid and Zaragoza. By the time he had served his sentence, late in 1874, he had received his diplomas of *licenciado* in philosophy and also in law. After a short visit to France and England, he settled in Mexico City early in 1875, together with his family, who had emigrated to that capital. There he remained until the revolt of Porfirio Díaz against the liberal government of Sebastián Lerdo de Tejada, in 1877, forced him into exile again. The two years that Martí lived in Mexico were very profitable for him. There his talent as a writer and poet matured. Through Mexico he discovered Latin America—his "magna patria," of which Cuba was only a small portion. "Our fatherland is one: it begins at the Rio Grande and ends in the muddy woodlands of Patagonia,"—he said in 1886.[1] There was a promising literary and ideological ferment in Mexico at the time, and the contact with the brilliant men of letters there was very stimulating for him. There he began his extraordinary journalistic career.

From Mexico he went to Guatemala, where he became professor of literature and philosophy. He was greatly admired and loved by his pupils, but the jealousy of small men around him, together with the despotic rule of President José Rufino Barrios, drove him from that Central American Republic in 1878.

The ten-year war for the liberation of Cuba had just ended in a truce, and the amnesty proclaimed by the Spanish crown on that occasion permitted Martí to return to his beloved fatherland. His only son was born during the few months of his stay in Havana. While in Cuba he earned his living working as a lawyer at the law office of two friends. The colonial government soon discovered his revolutionary activities and in 1879 again exiled him to Spain for an indefinite period. Martí escaped to France that very year, and after a few days in Paris, sailed for New York, where he arrived in January, 1880. The following February he began to publish a series of articles in English in the magazine *The Hour* and in July of the same year he started contributing to the *New York Sun,* a connection that lasted some twelve years. But life in the great metropolis was difficult for him and he decided to make one more attempt to settle in a less hostile climate and a more congenial social atmosphere. He went to Caracas, Venezuela, and tried to make a living by teaching. There he started the magazine *Revista Venezolana,* of which he was allowed to publish only two issues. As in Cuba, Mexico, and Guatemala, he was again, in Caracas, the victim of a despotic government, this time that of Antonio Guzmán Blanco, the dictatorial and vain ruler of Venezuela. Martí remained scrupulously aloof from local politics, but his natural gifts as orator and writer of high caliber as well as his unflinching devotion to freedom and democracy doomed him to inevitable conflict with the tyrant and to ultimate failure—unless he compromised. Soon he became the idol of the youth of Caracas, who flocked to his classes and public lectures on strictly cultural subjects. Furthermore, Martí had the temerity to publish a magnificent essay upon the death of the venerated Venezuelan humanist, Cecilio Acosta, the only intellectual residing in Caracas who had not submitted to the despot nor surrendered to him the freedom of his mind. This was too much for Guzmán Blanco, and Martí was confronted with the dilemma: either he would publish a similar eulogy of the autocrat, or he would have to leave the country. Rather than compromise his principles and conscience, Martí packed his meager belongings, wrote an admirable farewell letter to the Venezuelan people that enhanced his prestige, and took the first boat that sailed from La Guaira to New York.

Five times before he was thirty, Martí had been the victim of arbitrary rulers. Several times afterwards he renounced wealth, fame, and even his family rather than betray his conscience and his duty.[2] A less uncompromising attitude would have brought him wealth and social prominence. But between duty, honor, and personal dignity on the one hand, and prestige and money at the cost of conscience and self-respect, on the other, there was only one choice for him.

Very early in his life he discovered that material success and duty toward his fellow men—as he understood it—were incompatible. That is why he relinquished all claim to wealth and social importance which he could have had, preferring instead a humble life of service to mankind. In one of his best known short poems, he expressed his desire to affiliate himself with the unfortunate:

> With the needy of the earth
> Do I want my lot to cast....[3]

He returned to New York in 1881, poorer than when he left, but with his dignity intact and at peace with his conscience. His Venezuelan experience, though unhappy, was nevertheless very valuable and illuminating to him. His glimpse of another Spanish American country enriched his knowledge of the continent and convinced him of his duty to dedicate his life and efforts to the betterment of that turbulent part of the Americas which constituted his greater fatherland. To this ideal he devoted the rest of his life, with great generosity and fortitude. Except for short trips to Mexico, Central America, Santo Domingo, and Jamaica, always pursuant to his dream of liberating Cuba, he lived in New York until 1895, when he left for Cuba, where, on May 19 of that very year, he was to be killed fighting for the independence of the Island.

During the decade and a half that he lived in the United States, Martí worked for a time as a bookkeeper in a commercial concern, and for years as a translator for the publisher

D. Appleton and Company. In New York he published several journals, among others the best magazine for children that ever appeared in the Spanish language, entirely written by him.[4] He taught in the night schools of the city and for twelve years contributed articles to the *New York Sun*. He represented three Latin American countries, as consul of Argentina, Uruguay, and Paraguay in New York. He presided over several literary and cultural Latin American clubs or societies established in that city. In 1891 he was appointed delegate of Uruguay, with the rank of minister plenipotentiary, to the Pan American Monetary Commission held in Washington, and in it he played a decisive role. Until 1892 he was a regular columnist of, or a frequent contributor to, the most important newspapers of Spanish America, such as *La Opinión Nacional* of Caracas, *La Nación* of Buenos Aires, *El Partido Liberal* of Mexico, *La Opinión Pública* of Montevideo, and several others. Towards 1890 his intellectual and moral worth was universally recognized and acclaimed all through Spanish America—but, alas! not in his native Cuba. By this time, he had become a kind of cultural ambassador at large and spiritual symbol of the other America in New York.

Yet the most exhausting of all his enterprises and the one that gives us the measure of his mental caliber and practical capacity as a man of action was his founding and directing until his death of the Cuban Revolutionary Party. Into this organization he brought the Cubans living in exile and scattered all over the Atlantic coast from Key West to Boston, and in the Caribbean countries. For a period of ten years (1882-1892) of patient waiting and preparation, he educated the Cuban residents in the United States through his frequent lectures, his writings, and personal contacts. He kept the patriotic flame burning in their hearts. He instilled hope in the pessimist and courage in the pusillanimous; he inspired patriotic fervor in the indifferent and converted the most capable into active collaborators. All this time he scrutinized the policy of Spain toward Cuba and followed with increasing alarm the United States' diplomatic game with the crown of Spain regarding the final political destiny of the Island. It was in 1892, when he considered the moment ripe, that he founded the Revolutionary Party and assumed its leadership and responsibility.

Now began a heroic struggle in which he revealed himself as a true leader, and one of the greatest apostles of freedom that mankind has produced. He organized into a strictly democratic yet rigidly disciplined political party thousands of individualistic and quarrelsome Cubans. He collected regular weekly contributions from them. He persuaded the old and punctilious veteran generals to cooperate with one another and to recognize and accept the authority of the Party. He organized all the details of the revolution. He had to check the impatience of some and, at the same time, stimulate the laggards. He purchased, little by little, in absolute secrecy, always mindful of American neutrality laws and the perpetual vigilance of the secret agents, ships and armaments of all sorts and kept them hidden for many agonizing months. He had to keep up the fighting spirit of the patriots—those in exile as well as those inside the Island—and yet prevent all of them from jumping to a premature decision or from falling into the traps laid by the Spanish government and other opponents of Cuban independence. Such were some of the superhuman tasks that Martí performed during the last quinquennium of his life.

During the nearly fifteen years of his residence in New York his existence was a whirlwind of intellectual and political activity that astonishes and bewilders us today. He actually worked himself to death. His mental powers and physical endurance amaze us, especially if we remember that he always suffered from precarious health caused by the injuries received in jail in his adolescence. For years he suffered from an ailing heart and consumptive lungs. He was often bedridden, and in bed he frequently had to write and dispatch the most urgent matters. Toward the end of his life, he was so frail and physically depauperated, so thin and almost transparent, that he looked more like the ghost of a man than a living human being. So immaculate were the austerity of his life and the saintliness of his crusade and behavior when the final hour of decision approached, that people—particularly the humble —began to look upon him with reverence. Never had a revolutionary program and the preparation for a devastating war been organized with so much love and tenderness. So pure and self-sacrificing was his conduct, and so devoid of personal ambitions and egotism, that he finally won the hearts of all, imposed his moral authority upon his worst enemies, and converted to his creed the most recalcitrant adversaries.

Here is the testimony of two distinguished Americans who knew him well. Charles Anderson Dana was one of the most prominent figures produced by American journalism. As editor of the *New York Sun* he made this paper one of the most respected and influential organs of public opinion in this country during the last quarter of the nineteenth century. For many years, Dana had been a friend and admirer of Martí, whose collaboration in the *Sun* he had requested. When the cable brought to him the sad news of Martí's death, Dana wrote this fervent obituary in his paper:

"We learn with poignant sorrow of the death in battle of JOSÉ MARTÍ, the well-known leader of Cuban revolutionists. We knew him long and well, and esteemed him profoundly. For a protracted period, beginning twenty-odd years ago,[5] he was employed as a contributor to THE SUN, writing on subjects and questions of the fine arts. In these things his learning was solid and extensive, and his ideas and conclusions were original and brilliant. He was a man of genius, of imagination, of hope, and of courage, one of those descendants of the SPANISH race whose American birth and instincts seemed to have added to the revolutionary tincture which all modern Spaniards inherit. His heart was warm and affectionate, his opinions ardent and aspiring, and he died as such a man might wish to die, battling for liberty and democracy. Of such heroes there are not too many in the world, and his warlike grave testifies that, even in a positive and material age, there are spirits that can give all for their principles without thinking of any selfish return for themselves.

"Honor to the memory of JOSÉ MARTÍ, and peace to his manly and generous soul!"[6]

The second testimony is that of Horace S. Rubens, a distinguished lawyer, who for years was in charge of the legal department of the Cuban Revolutionary Party and later represented the Cuban revolution in all the legal conflicts with the laws of the United States and its policy toward Cuba. Describing the first impression that Martí produced on him, Rubens wrote:

"In that moment I knew I had never seen a more magnetic man, never perhaps even imagined a man of so extraordinary a personality."[7]

The American historian, Willis Fletcher Johnson, attests to the genius and apostolic qualities of Martí. He described Martí's role as organizer of Cuba's War of Independence in the following words:

"The foremost director of that war, its organizer and inspirer, was José Martí; one of those rare geniuses who have appeared occasionally in the history of the world to be the incarnation of great ideals of justice and human right. He was indeed many times a genius: Organizer, economist, historian, poet, statesman, tribune of the people, apostle of freedom, above all, Man. In himself he united the virtues, the enthusiasm and the energizing vitality which his countrymen needed to have aroused in themselves. To his disorganized and disheartened country he brought a magic personality which won all hearts and inspired them with all his own irrepressible and indestructible ideal, National Independence." [8]

Paraphrasing his own perfect epitaph of Emerson, we may also say that in Martí man attained the highest degree of dignity.

Man of Culture and Ideals

A DISTINGUISHED humanist of Columbia University wrote some time ago that the life of Martí "was one of the most intense, pure and noble that ever existed on the earth."[1] But the intellectual in him, the man of culture and ideals, as well as the thinker, was as great as the man himself. It is not easy to understand how Martí could find time to read so extensively in the midst of the turmoil of activity that was his life in New York. Yet in the seventy-volume edition in which his writings have been collected, we find ample proof of his broad culture. He was widely read in literature, history, philosophy, and many other subjects. He was familiar with the Greek and Roman classics and with European culture, whether English or German, French or Italian. He was equally interested in music and followed the trends of painting in the United States and Europe with a keen and ever alert interest. How he could accomplish so much remains a mystery.

José Martí was one of the most brilliant and original prose writers of all time. He was also a poet of note, but much more "a poet of action." His poetic gifts are as evident in his prose as in his poems, and nowhere more patent than in his epistolary. The rich collection of his private letters, of which more than six hundred have been published, constitutes one of the most fascinating expressions of his powerful individuality and literary genius. It is the only aspect of his extensive writings in which we can appreciate all the manifestations of his multilateral personality: the warmth and tenderness of his heart, his infinite capacity for love and sympathy, his catholicity, his noble ideals, his vigorous—and sometimes exquisitely charming—style as a writer, his poetic qualities, his refinement of spirit and manners.

He was also an exceptional thinker without being what is commonly called a philosopher. He had little use for purely speculative thinking. He was more concerned with this world, particularly with mankind and its betterment, than with abstract or metaphysical speculation. To a certain extent, he could be called a pragmatist, but he can hardly be classified as a loyal disciple or follower of any school of philosophy, with the possible exception of the Stoic system. Stoic he certainly was, though more by temperament and behavior than by any process of ratiocination. As William Rex Crawford pointed out some years ago: "... he was also an artist and an intellect fertile in ideas. Ideas were for him weapons in the fight for a better world, in which freedom for Cuba was the first step. To preach this gospel and to redeem America, this was his obsession and his mission." [2]

It would be interesting—and very illuminating—to compare here the ideology of Martí with that of Ralph Waldo Emerson, for whom Martí had unbounded admiration, and about whom he wrote a penetrating essay on the occasion of his death. There is a striking similarity between the two in many respects, notwithstanding the cultural, religious, and individual peculiarities that separate them. In spite of Emerson's violent reaction against many prejudices, traditions, and intolerances of his New England, he is a typical product of his cultural, social, and religious environment and of his times. So is Martí of his. Both epitomized and symbolized the finest human values of their respective peoples. But we find in Martí a warmth and tenderness, a capacity for compassion and sacrifice, a predisposition to serve and to redeem his fellow men which were lacking in Emerson—at least to the same degree. Emerson was more the man of thought; Martí was more apostolic, more fervent in his consuming love of mankind. Both were contemplative; but while the New Englander remained happy in his meditations, Martí yearned for a better world, longed for a more equitable and just social and economic order, and struggled and died fighting for his ideals. Nevertheless, in the history of American thought few men could be found whose ideas about nature and society offer a closer analogy to those of Martí.

When one realizes the multiplicity of mental and spiritual powers in Martí—the orator, thinker, poet, prose writer, political leader, statesman, apostle of freedom—and analyzes the high degree of perfection which all of these qualities reached in him, one is really astounded. Few men in history have been so generously endowed. Yet what is most admirable in him is the perfect unity and fullness of his personality, the harmonious completeness and integration of his being. In vain do we look for a flaw in his character or in his life. One may disagree with his philosophy or dislike his personal style as a writer, but among the thousands of books, pamphlets, and articles written about him, in three continents, no writer has failed to express almost reverent admiration for that consummate blending of unblemished moral qualities with supreme intellectual faculties which formed his unique personality. The man of action and the man of thought were so perfectly blended in him that one hesitates to venture a classification. Like Cervantes, Martí himself considered action more worthy and fruitful than mere words—whether written or spoken. In his infinite love of humanity, he once wrote: "Only the men of deeds remain; and above all the men whose deeds were guided by love. Only love penetrates and endures.... Only love builds." [3]

One of the few North American critics acquainted with Martí's life and writings—the first one, perhaps, to discover him—aptly defined his personality in 1920 with the following words: "A remarkable union of the man of contemplation and the man of action, a vagrant pioneer in both mind and body, an innovator in language because of the new vision he beheld, Martí is enshrined in both the literature and the history of his people. His life was as noble as his writings; he died for that to which he had devoted his life, and Cuba is his monument." [4]

He had unbounded love for humanity and blind faith in the final triumph of goodness over evil in the heart of men. "Man is ugly, but mankind is beautiful," he said once, suggesting the idea that notwithstanding individual exceptions, mankind as a whole is generous and kind. Many of us will wonder at such an optimistic conclusion, which probably reflects more his own philanthropy and benevolence rather than an objective reality. In a recent article in the *New York Times*, Abel Plenn wrote: "Indeed, his exaltation of that love for humanity frequently transcends the humanism not only of the eighteenth and nineteenth century thought but of our own country as well, and makes him seem more like a spokesman of some future civilization.... [He was] a poet-philosopher who forced himself to become a fighter for oppressed humanity. For Martí, involved as he was in the immediate political fate of his native Cuba and other Latin American countries, was even more profoundly concerned with the lot of all mankind." [5]

Man of Destiny

IN TIMES of great social or political changes or crises every country which is not already decadent, produces the man —or men—that incarnates the aspirations and needs of his people. These are the founders and leaders, the heroes and apostles of the new ideals and the builders of the new society.[1] The French and American revolutions in the eighteenth century, the Spanish American revolution of independence, and the Russian revolution of 1917, are cases in point. George Washington, Thomas Jefferson, Mirabeau, Robespierre, Bolívar, Lincoln, Juárez, Cavour, Martí, Lenin, Gandhi and Franklin D. Roosevelt are some of the great men of destiny that mankind has produced in the last two centuries. Martí belongs in this category. In more than one way he was superior to most of his historical peers, but the small size of his native land has deprived him of that economic, military, and cultural pedestal that a large country always affords to its great men. When projected into an international perspective, the importance of the fatherland accrues to the actual merits and virtues of a leader and magnifies and enhances his reputation. On the other hand, if a man of equal or superior mental and moral stature happens to be born in a little country, its international insignificance detracts from his due fame, retards and even precludes recognition abroad, and weighs upon him and usually reduces him to the rank of a local hero.

Such is not exactly the case of Martí, for while the North American intelligentsia have ignored him—or rather have known practically nothing about him—he has been acclaimed a genius and a hero in the Spanish-speaking world and by French, German, and Italian writers. For many he was also a kind of lay saint. In spite of his birth on an island, his repute has transcended the boundaries of Spanish culture—a fact that attests to his true greatness. If he has failed to gain recognition in the intellectual circles of the United States, it is due to its cultural provincialism and its proclivity to confuse bigness with greatness, or to interpret the latter in terms of the former.

In the case of Martí, the surprising fact is that a little country of less than two million inhabitants at the time should have produced such an intellectual and moral giant. But the anomaly becomes easily understandable when we project him into the vastness of Spanish America and consider him a continental leader—which he truly was—rather than an insular one. For Martí and his apostolic career actually belong to the whole Spanish-speaking world as much as to Cuba. If he concentrated his efforts on liberating his native island and Puerto Rico, it was not because he was narrowly nationalistic, but because these were the only two Spanish colonies in America still unredeemed and, particularly Cuba, in serious danger of being annexed by the United States.

Martí always wrote and acted in terms of Spanish America. The very liberation of Cuba was in his conception an act of serving the other America—"our America," as he used to call it, to differentiate it from the United States. His spirit was too universal and the scope of his ideals too broad to be contained within the isolating borders of any country. More than a Cuban citizen he was actually a knight-errant of liberty and freedom who never ceased to fight for them until he died. He fought Spanish and Spanish American despots, and as soon as he discovered the expansionist tendency of certain economic interests in the United States and the imperialistic ambitions of some of its political leaders, he combated both with unabated zeal and energy. Years before "manifest destiny" became openly imperialistic and the United States began to tread upon its neighbor's sovereignty, Martí foresaw the danger and warned "his America" in a ceaseless crusade, which lasted over fifteen years and which Latin America—much to its regret—did not heed.

He was ever alert and disposed to defend Spanish American dignity and rights, always ready to battle in their defense. At the very moment when United States policy towards its neighbors was about to change, and long before it became peremptory and aggressive, Martí saw the handwriting on the Latin American wall and became the prophet and champion of that unfortunate continent. He was always ready to battle against injustice and oppression, against the abuse and exploitation of the weak by the powerful, regardless of race or country, color or class interest. Mankind was one, for him, and universal were the greed and avarice of the potentates—whether individual or country—that produced the equally universal misery and suffering of the vast majority everywhere. He felt in his own heart the moans of the needy, the oppressed and despoiled, and he answered the call and fought in their defense all his life. Contemplating with indignation the miserable life of the working class in New York, he wrote in 1886: "He who can observe the deplorable life of today's wretched workingman and woman in these cold latitudes without feeling his soul wrenched with pity, is not only basely insensitive, but commits a criminal act. It is man's duty to uplift his fellow man. We are guilty of every human degradation that we do not strive to remedy."[2]

If the situation had been reversed and the United States had been the weak nation and Cuba or Latin America the oppressing power, he would have struggled with equal fervor and heroism in defense of the United States against the abusive country. Justice and freedom were indivisible for him. In spite of his intense patriotism, he would never have endorsed the doctrine of "my country, right or wrong." Such a creed would have been repugnant and barbarous to him, proper only to primitive tribes.

We see now why he was a man of fate, not only for Cuba but for the whole Latin American continent. When the fateful hour struck, when their respective destinies were about to undergo a transcendent change, and both were confronted by a serious danger, Martí became the symbol and the spokesman of his people. He forged the future of his native land by forcing the war of liberation upon her before the United States had time to come to an agreement with Spain to annex it. Martí was much more afraid of Washington's covetous plans regarding Cuba than he was of Spanish military power. Referring to the imperialistic interests of Wall Street and to the super-patriots who clamored for the conquest or annexation of new territories, he condensed in one metaphorical sentence, contained in an unfinished letter to a friend, his purpose in setting Cuba on fire in February of 1895. Casting himself in the role of David, and the United States tacitly in that of the giant Goliath in the Biblical drama, he wrote on May 18, 1895, the day before he died: "I know the monster because I have lived in its lair, and my sling is that of David."[3]

The United States in the Eighties

THE FIFTEEN YEARS that Martí lived in New York constitute a period of tremendous transformation in the economic life of the United States and, consequently, in its social structure. By 1880, when he arrived, the country had already recovered, to a large extent, from the material devastation caused by the Civil War. The economy was still mainly rural, with the emphasis on railroad-building, mining, timber, and cattle-raising. The colonization and exploitation of new territories, snatched from the Indians, and the wilderness of the Far West had not been completed by any means. As yet the United States was a debtor country, and foreign capital was still pouring in to help in the development of its wealth and natural resources. Heavy industry and manufacturing in general were still trailing England's, but already were making rapid strides.

The torrent of immigration, which since the end of the Civil War had flooded the country, reached new levels. Between 1880 and 1895, many millions of hardworking German, Polish, Czech, Scandinavian, Irish, Russian, Italian, and Jewish immigrants entered the United States and contributed their skill, their energy, and their technical knowledge to the rapid material progress of the country. The population of the United

States increased rapidly during these fifteen years—and so did the national wealth. It was an epoch of terrific economic development and social ferment, of rapid transformation from an economy primarily rural to one in which heavy industry, banking, manufacturing, and commerce predominated as the century drew to a close. These years at the end of the century marked the culmination of a democratic experiment, of capitalistic expansion, of rugged individualism. During these years the frontier spirit not only invaded the plains and forests of the West, but also permeated the country's political life and all phases of its business. The motto was "Each man for himself," in a pitiless struggle in which the most ruthless and brutal was usually the most successful. It was a kind of jungle-like strife in which ethical principles were badly neglected. But it was also epic and even beautiful, virile, healthy, and somehow sporting—as Walt Whitman has depicted it. It was the greatest experiment that mankind had witnessed in political democracy and capitalistic freedom to exploit nature and human energy.

The positivist philosophical school prevalent at the time in the occidental world, justified "the survival of the fittest," and, as interpreted by some, even condoned the exploitation of the feeble by the strong. Supported by this distorted social philosophy, the enterprising and energetic individual, as well as the corporations of the industrial centers, exploited the great masses of workers with the same ruthlessness practiced by the railroad barons, the big ranchers, or the coal mining operators. The social irresponsibility and the moral callousness of the industrial entrepreneurs of the time were shameful demonstrations of the cruelty of man toward man in a country that claimed adherence to the principles of Christianity. The philosophy of the plutocracy of the eighties in regard to labor was perfectly expressed by the railroad king, Jay Gould—whom Martí denounced on several occasions—in the following sentence: "Labor is a *commodity* [emphasis mine] that will in the long run be governed absolutely by the law of supply and demand."[1] In the minds of these most Christian gentlemen, labor was "a commodity" whose price should be governed by the same law that determines that of cattle, coal, or potatoes. The inevitable consequence was the dramatic social turmoil of the times: the epic and bloody strikes, the emergence of a class-conscious proletariat and the ineluctable sequel of social fermentation, legal as well as political repercussions, and stern repressions.

The economic evolution that took place in the United States during the years 1880-1895, affected in a decisive way its foreign policy. By the end of the century there had already accumulated a surplus of capital products of all kinds that the domestic market could not absorb. Hence the expansionist demands, and the eagerness with which some political leaders advocated a frankly imperialist policy. They simply reflected the need of new markets for excess products and new investment opportunities for the financial plethora. The economic transformation and the concomitant change in foreign policy were intimately related and determined by the law of cause and effect.

Martí, Chronicler of Transformation

WHEN MARTÍ finally settled in New York in 1881, he decided to earn his living by writing. Conscious of the fast growing international importance of the United States, and mindful of the urgent need of Latin America for a clear and realistic picture—and understanding—of this country, he resolved to become the interpreter of North American history and culture, politics, and national character. By doing so, he would render an invaluable service to the other America. Pursuant to this educational aim, he set himself to the task of studying the history and traditions of the United States, its national idiosyncrasies and institutions. At the same time he would observe with eager eyes contemporary life in all its infinite manifestations. So earnest and persevering was his desire to familiarize himself with the historical background and present-day society and culture, that within one year after his arrival he was writing competently on practically any subject pertaining to our country.

His first reaction upon his arrival was one of amazement at, and great admiration for, the new world he was discovering—so original, so complex, and so totally different from any other country he had visited. To a certain extent, he never ceased to wonder at the spectacle of North American life, at the dynamic character of its people, at the freedom that everybody enjoyed to preach any creed or to propagate new ideas and ideals. Freedom and tolerance were then cardinal virtues of American social and political philosophy, now, unfortunately, fast disappearing. The ruling classes of the last quarter of the century had more faith in the vitality of democracy than we have today. Men were not persecuted then for what they thought or for their associations, but for what they did. As former Attorney General Francis Biddle puts it: "During the nineteenth century censorship was practically unknown; men were not prosecuted for their utterances; they were allowed to associate with any organization they pleased. Words with a radical tendency were not punished." [1]

One can easily imagine Martí's admiration for the freedom he saw in the United States, if we remember his sad experiences with despotic governments. The dignity of the individual, in whose defense he struggled all his life, was the cornerstone of American political doctrine and constitutional law. Although in practice this principle was not always honored by the authorities and courts, no other country up to that time had adhered to it so consistently in theory, or had endeavoured more tenaciously to make it the basis of the relationships between citizen and government or individual and corporations. This exaltation of the human being, consecrated in the political thinking and in the positive law of this country, coupled with the devotion to freedom and liberty, were romantic and idealistic notions that coincided perfectly with Martí's ideals. The dignity of man is the main concept on which rests his political and social philosophy. It is a leitmotiv that, like an obsession, recurs a thousand times in his writings. It is succinctly and admirably expressed in the definition of liberty which he wrote for the children of Latin America: "Liberty," he said, "is the right that every man possesses to be honest, and to think and to speak without hypocrisy." [2] Hence the enthusiasm with which he always extolled this peculiarity of the national life of the United States. There is no other facet of its culture so intensely admired by him as this tendency in its legislation to elevate and to dignify the human being. In 1885 he wrote:

"You will know an infamous man by his abuse of the humble men. The weak should be sacred for us, as the insane were for the ancient Greeks. He who takes pleasure in humbling another human being, attests to his own base character. There is an aristocracy of the spirit: it is formed by those who rejoice in the growth and affirmation of man. The human species has but one cheek: wherever a man is struck on his cheek, every man receives the blow." [3]

Equipped with a solid knowledge of the history of the United States, and familiar with the contemporary scene, Martí began to interpret their northern neighbor to his Latin American readers. His extraordinary talent, his poetic and plastic imagination, his sense of fairness and responsibility made of him an ideal chronicler, the most remarkable, perhaps, of all the foreigners who have written about this country. In the seventy-volume collection of his complete works, his essays dealing with the United States fill seventeen volumes. He actually rediscovered this nation for Spanish America. His first chronicles were published in *La Opinión Nacional* of Caracas in 1881, but soon thereafter he began contributing to *La Nación* of Buenos Aires, to *La Opinión Pública* of Montevideo, *El Partido Liberal* of Mexico City, and occasionally to several other journals. So interesting and illuminating were his articles, and so popular did they become throughout

Spanish America that soon more than twenty daily journals were reproducing them in different countries.[4]

Three generations of Latin American readers have learned, in his writings, to admire United States institutions, great men, and noble traditions. None of the many Spanish American intellectuals who have written on this country even approaches Martí's epic description or his sagacious essays on famous American writers and public figures. This ponderous mass of literature is journalistic only to the extent that it was written for, and originally published in, the Spanish American newspapers. A large part of it is necessarily impressionistic and fragmentary—like all literary production destined to appear in the daily press—but not ephemeral. Collected in book form, it is read throughout Spanish America today with the same eagerness with which it was read in the newspapers sixty years ago. It would be difficult to find, in the annals of any newspaper, articles more saturated with ideas, more illuminating, or written in a more original and vigorous style. Journalism has never reached a higher degree of dignity or achieved a nobler goal.

Trying to explain his inability to write frivolously or without conviction, Martí said in a letter to the editor of *La Nación* of Buenos Aires in 1882: "It is a defect in me to be unable to create anything in fragments, to wish to saturate with essence even small works, and to conceive newspaper articles as if they were books.... There is no greater torment for me than to write against the soul or without it."[5]

What he called his "defect" is precisely what made his journalistic production so inimitable and so enduring. There is not a page or a letter of this prolific writer in which we could not discover unusual aesthetic qualities, together with ideological or ethical values. Unfortunately, his prose is one of the most difficult to render into English that could be found in the Hispanic world.

For more than a decade Martí covered every significant political or international event that took place in the United States. A good many American public men and intellectuals died during that time, and Martí immortalized them in Spanish in a long series of famous obituaries that are still eagerly read today. He described in a torrential prose natural phenomena like the Charleston earthquake of 1886; the momentous works wrought by men, like the Brooklyn Bridge and the Statue of Liberty; the bloody strikes; the religious conflicts; the commemoration of great historical events such as the first centennial of the Congress of Philadelphia or the founding of a town in a few hours in the West; student life in colleges and the system of education; economic policies and political campaigns; the great virtues and great defects of the people of the United States. No aspect of its national life or character was too insignificant for him to comment upon.

Because he was truly great and pure of mind and spirit, he could admire and exalt everything that was worthy of praise and admiration in its history and contemporary society. He found in this country great men, noble traditions, and institutions to commend and to revere. No other writer has ever described its best national traits, its love of freedom, or its struggle for the dignity of man, with more ardent fervor or in more eloquent words. But he also hated greed and selfishness, corruption and petty passions, and petty individuals. He detested the professional patriots, and corrupt politicians who served vested interests rather than the people who elected them. He had an unbearable contempt for the political chicanery practiced in his time by both parties and their respective leaders and "machines," denouncing them time and again with scorn and indignation. As we shall see presently, he revolted at the way in which both parties bought and sold and traded votes on election days as they would trade goods in the market place.[6]

A Plutarchian Portrayer

THE SECOND arrival of José Martí in New York in August, 1881, coincided very closely with the criminal assault against President Garfield which put an end to his life a few weeks later. With this tragic event as a subject, José Martí began his contributions to Spanish American journals on August 20, 1881. He followed the prolonged agony of the martyred President with deep sympathy and shared in the nation's grief during the weeks that separated the fatal shooting from the actual death. He wrote extensively on President Garfield. Martí's generous spirit and his sympathy and admiration for the fortitude with which the victim endured suffering made his portrayal of Garfield extremely benevolent and perhaps too idealistic. It was written in a moment of national sorrow and he meant every word he wrote.[1]

With the study of Garfield begins his long series of essays on political figures. Both Ralph Waldo Emerson and Henry W. Longfellow died in 1882, a few months after the President succumbed. On these occasions Martí wrote the first of his critical studies on American men of letters. Up to that moment, cultural relations between the United States and Latin America were practically nonexistent. The lack of interest—and ignorance—had been reciprocal. Martí took it upon himself to reveal to his people the literary values of their northern neighbor. He chose for his first topic the most original and robust thinker the United States had produced, and, for his second, the most popular of its contemporary poets.

Martí's essay on Emerson was the first of a series on that famous poet-philosopher published in Spanish. It still stands out as one of the most powerful syntheses ever written on the Sage of Concord. It was a great revelation for his readers, and demonstrated the close ideological and ethical affinity of the two men. The following paragraph attests to the fidelity of Martí's interpretation and to the reverence with which he regarded Emerson. Unfortunately, it is not possible to translate the captivating beauty of the original.

"He was tender towards men and loyal to himself. They had educated him to teach one creed, yet he passed on to the credulous his preacher's coat, feeling that he wore upon his shoulders the august mantle of Nature. Obedience to any system was from his viewpoint proper only to blind men and slaves; nor did he create one, for this seemed to him the course of weak, shallow, and envious minds. He submerged himself in Nature, and emerged radiant. He felt himself a man, and by reason of that, God. He wrote of what he knew, and if unable to observe, he remained silent. He revealed what he perceived, and venerated what was beyond his perception. He looked into the Universe with his own eyes, and spoke a language of his own. He was a creator by not wishing to be one. He felt divine raptures and lived in gratifying and celestial contemplations. He knew the ineffable sweetness of ecstasy. His mind was not for hire, nor his pen, nor his conscience. Like a star, he radiated light. In him the human being attained the highest degree of dignity." [2]

On Henry W. Longfellow he wrote twice, once before his

death early in 1882, and later a magnificent obituary when the poet passed away. Both articles are equally beautiful and revealing of the lofty ideals of the poet and of his unblemished life. Of the man Longfellow, Martí wrote:

"How perfect was his life! He possessed that mystic dignity proper of the noble souls. He had the healthy color of the pure; the magnificent pride of the virtuous; the generosity of the great; the melancholy of those still alive, and that longing for death that makes life beautiful." [3]

The most outstanding, perhaps, of all his critical essays on American men of letters, was the one he devoted to Walt Whitman in 1887. As in the case of Oscar Wilde, Emerson, Longfellow, and so many other great European and American contemporaries, he introduced Whitman to his readers. Very few Latin American poets or writers were acquainted with the author of *Leaves of Grass* in the eighties, and none had attempted to interpret his poetry. Even in the United States, Whitman was still considered something of a reprobate by churches and moral societies. *Leaves of Grass* was still anathema and its circulation through the mail still prohibited. Only among the literary elite was Whitman recognized as a great poet when Martí wrote his study.

The healthy pantheism of Whitman, his love for humanity, his mystic feeling of brotherhood, his pagan or Bacchic attitude toward life and nature, his delight in freedom and liberty, his almost religious exaltation of democracy, his scorn at, and defiance of, all forms of conventionalism and bigotry, his Biblical and unique style, found in Martí an admirable interpreter. Although many Spanish critics and poets have since written on Whitman, Martí's essay still remains the one most worthy of the poet in the Spanish language. This study was simultaneously published in both Mexico and Buenos

Aires and provoked earnest interest in Whitman among the literati of the continent and gave impetus to studies and translations of his poems.

Martí also introduced for the first time to the Spanish reading public many other important and minor personalities of American literature and historiography. Among them were Washington Irving, Mark Twain, William Prescott, George Bancroft, Bronson Alcott and his daughter, Louisa May, the Quaker poet Whittier, Helen Hunt Jackson, whose *Ramona* he rendered beautifully into Spanish, and many others.

Another aspect of our culture never explored by Spanish American writers or critics before Martí was painting. For the first time in the Spanish language, Martí evaluated for Spanish Americans, in many articles and short references, the plastic arts—particularly painting—in the United States. He was deeply interested in this form of artistic expression and was familiar with its history and contemporary manifestations in both Europe and the Americas. At the same time that he propagated knowledge of the artistic progress of this country in Spanish America, he contributed to the esthetic education of North Americans. During the twelve years of his connection with the *New York Sun*, he kept the readers of that paper constantly informed of the European evolution in the field of plastic arts.

Equal in caliber to his critical studies of the men of letters, are his searching character sketches of prominent civic leaders of the day. Most of these men distinguished themselves for their integrity and noble qualities, for their profound sense of social responsibility, and for the tenacity and valor with which they fought to defend their ideals. Most of them advocated unpopular causes. None submitted to what is called "group thinking," "group psychology," or "group prejudices and fanaticism." They were truly free and great men who struggled heroically, sometimes against the bigotry and stupidity prevalent in their social environment. Martí admired these rebels heartily. In them he saw perfect examples of the ideal citizens of a free and democratic republic. Their respective lives and courage inspired some of his best psychological and biographical studies. Because none of these venerable abolitionists and rebellious defenders of freedom and social justice occupied important political positions, history has practically forgotten them, and the youth of today in the United States, hardly knows who they were. In Spanish America, on the other hand, thanks to Martí's writings, the memory of these men is still very much alive.

Among the abolitionists, none was more admired by Martí than Wendell Phillips. This Bostonian was an aristocrat in blood and wealth, but even more in spirit and deeds. Wendell Phillips was an apostle of abolition and social reforms who consecrated his life to these ideals. He preached his crusade with great fervor and eloquence. He was a lawyer by training and vocation, but he never practised his profession, because to do so he would have had to sign an oath upholding the constitution. Since the Constitution seemed to sanction the ignominy of slavery, he refused to take the constitutional oath and devoted his life to the task of erasing that blot from American history. With unflinching bravery and fiery words he defied the prejudices and the animosity of the masses, the bitter opposition of those who profited from slavery and defended it, and the threats of his enemies. Nobody during the thirty years preceding the Civil War was a more ardent, unselfish, and eloquent crusader than Wendell Phillips. Nobody, afterwards, struggled more tenaciously and more generously against the forces of greed and the sanctity of wealth. With uncommon courage he denounced to the end of his life the avarice and the injustices of plutocracy, and consecrated himself to the defense of the humble and the despoiled. In his altruistic wrath, he may have erred or lost sight of the realities and possibilities of his time, but as R. H. Tawney says, "When to speak is unpopular, it is less pardonable to be silent than to say too much." [4] On the occasion of Phillips' death, in 1884, Martí wrote three articles. The last two in particular constitute a fervid tribute to that most extraordinary man and orator, whose life and character in so many ways resembled those of Martí.[5]

To the group of great abolitionists also belonged Henry Ward Beecher, a most remarkable Protestant minister. Though less cultured and not so perfect an orator as Phillips, he was nonetheless a persevering and devoted combatant in the glorious struggle. Martí had little use for organized religion or for mere church men of any denomination. In Henry Ward Beecher, what he admired and extolled were not the attributes of the preacher but the sterling qualities of the man and his philanthropic endeavors.[6]

Martí did not approve of vast fortunes. The idea of a man's accumulating wealth at the expense of masses of workers who lacked the bare necessities of life was repugnant to him. The spectacle of so much misery existing side by side with so much ostentatious luxury seemed to him a social crime. We find it denounced time and again in his writings. In 1883, exactly fifty years before the inauguration of the New Deal, Martí propounded the same social philosophy when, referring to the poverty of the proletarian districts of New York, he wrote: "And I say that this is a public crime, and that it is the duty of the state to put an end to unnecessary misery." [7]

Nevertheless, Martí did not condemn the acquisition of

wealth by honest means. What he repudiated was the idea of elevating the conquest of material success to the rank of an ideal, and the admiration prevalent in American society for those who achieve it regardless of the means employed. He had only scorn for what he called the "cult of wealth" in the United States. Thus he stigmatized it in 1888:

"... the disproportionate craving for material wealth, the scorn for those who have not acquired it, and the servile admiration for those who obtain it, even though at the cost of their honor or by criminal means, brutalizes and corrupts nations. Without question, those who favor or practice the cult of wealth should be denied social esteem and considered an insidious and destructive force within the country, like an infection, or like Shakespeare's Iago. It is admirable to acquire wealth by honest and vigorous labor, its accumulation by destructive or deceitful means which dishonor those who employ them and corrupt the nation in which they are practiced, is palpable proof of moral turpitude and shamelessness, and a crime worthy of legal punishment. The rich, like thoroughbred horses, should have the pedigree of their wealth where everyone can view it." [8]

He had as much contempt for those who accumulate wealth at the expense of others as he had admiration for some of the philanthropic millionaires who used their riches to improve the lot of the less fortunate. One of those rare specimens was Peter Cooper, great industrialist, inventor, and benefactor of mankind. Martí had almost reverent admiration for him. Not even Emerson inspired a more ardent obituary from his pen than did Peter Cooper at the time of his death in 1883. Notice the filial veneration with which he begins the essay:

"Flags are at half mast; hearts grieve: Peter Cooper is dead. He leaves behind thousands of grateful and devoted workers.

I was not born in this land, nor did he ever know me. Yet, I loved him as a father. If ever our paths had crossed, I would have kissed his hand." [9]

Another millionaire who merited Martí's admiration was Courtlandt Palmer, one of the most eccentric members of New York's aristocracy in the eighties. Palmer was a passionate lover and defender of freedom in the broadest meaning of the word. He advocated not only political freedom, but freedom to think, to believe or not to believe—in God or anything else. He was called the "socialist millionaire" because of his humanitarian ideals and because he would invite socialist and anarchist thinkers to lecture in the debating academy which he founded. He himself was an atheist, but he would invite ministers and priests of all creeds to expound their respective philosophies side by side with agnostics and atheists. Courtlandt Palmer was not afraid of so-called subversive ideas, nor did he refuse the rostrum of his debating society to those who preached revolutionary doctrines. For him culture and society were not static or stagnant organisms, but dynamic, perpetually evolving, ever changing; and whenever culture and society cease to renovate themselves by mutating and assimilating new ideals and goals, they decay and die. Palmer, although very rich, was not afraid of change. His home was actually a temple without liturgy or theology, in which all social, political, philosophical, or religious gospels could be preached. He believed only in one religion: the brotherhood of man. Palmer was a devoted disciple of Auguste Comte and his positivistic school. Martí was the opposite, but he had a profound admiration for the sincerity, the courage, and the moral and intellectual integrity of Palmer and wrote a sympathetic panegyric upon his death in 1888.

It does not come within the scope of this brief study to give a full account of the importance of José Martí's articles analyzing public men and the political panorama of his times. They constitute the most valuable aspect of his voluminous reporting about the United States. Here will be given only a brief résumé of his keen judgments of public leaders and his realistic analysis of political life in the eighties.

Martí was attracted first by the personalities that dominated both parties in his day. We have already seen how he began with a series of articles in which he reported minutely the process of President Garfield's struggle for life, and climaxed them with a biographical and psychological study of the man and his importance in the politics of his time. Martí had an almost religious reverence for the great North American leaders of the past, particularly for Thomas Paine, George Washington, Thomas Jefferson and Abraham Lincoln. He wrote several times about Washington, and though no extensive articles on the other three can be found in his writings, he made hundreds of admiring references to them.

But he was more concerned with contemporary politics and politicians than with historical heroes. He set himself to study the intricacies and intrigues of public life in the United States, and the shoddy economic interests that, behind the curtain, manipulated the politicians of his time. It is astonishing to discover what a profound knowledge he had of the corruption and chicanery prevalent in his day. We must remember that those were the post-Grant administration years in which big business controlled the government and bribed legislators and executives to obtain advantageous and unlawful concessions. Never in the history of the country had corruption in public life reached such scandalous proportions as between 1870 and 1890. Martí witnessed this pernicious influence of big business in public affairs, and also the healthy reaction initiated during the first administration of Grover Cleveland. He recorded both in a long series of vivid articles that constitute today an excellent source of information on the political mores and men of that period.

The two dominant figures of the Republican party at the time that Martí began to write on contemporary political activity, never realized their presidential aspirations. Both are almost forgotten today, but their reciprocal hostility, their implacable rivalry, and their intrigues against each other dominated the policy of the party for years, and decided the political fortunes of many a minor personality. They were Roscoe Conkling, Senator from New York, lawyer, great orator, and powerful leader, who fully controlled his home state, and James G. Blaine of Maine, brilliant, skillful, and equally powerful. They were two giant contenders who never compromised or surrendered their respective ambitions to the advantage of the other. The consequence of this animosity between Blaine and Conkling was the nomination of James A. Garfield and Chester A. Arthur in the Republican convention of 1880. Both Conkling and Blaine were carefully studied by Martí, as we shall see presently.

Martí did not write his penetrating analysis of President Arthur until 1886, when Garfield's running mate and successor died. It is one of the best biographical and psychological sketches he ever wrote. Here his epigrammatic and aphoristic style found perfect expression. It is a much more realistic portrayal than that of Garfield. Martí never deprived any of the men he portrayed of the credit due them. Thus, in the following paragraphs, he depicts perfectly both the astute politician and the urbane man that Arthur was:

"The history of Arthur's political career is to be found in the intrigues of his party. He never progressed or advanced by himself and because of his own merits, but as a representative of the clique he served within the party.

"None of his defeats or triumphs, none of his notable achievements, is a national event in which great ideas clash or are controverted. They are a mere product of intraparty squabbles in which the rival personalities ravage one another's gains and reputation.

"Once in office, it is true, he would win the good will of everybody through his gentlemanly moderation, his suave way of tempering his energy, his sincere kindness, and, above all, through his gracious and courteous manners and dignified simplicity, which enhance personal merit and sometimes simulate it or substitute for it.

"But if he was affectionate with his subordinates and irreproachable in his handling of public funds, he never failed to take advantage of the influence with which these very acts provided him. Gradually he wove such a strong and tightly knit political organization that throughout the state there was not a single district without an agent employed by him, nor a convention in which his candidates did not emerge triumphant, nor an intrigue possible without his consent, nor an election assured except through his intervention...."[10]

"He did not sacrifice his honesty to his ambition. This was his glory in the desolation of his political catastrophe...he died celebrated for his personal charms, and for having redeemed himself."[11]

Among Martí's most enduring biographical studies is the one he devoted to General Ulysses S. Grant upon his death in 1885. Grant's military career and achievements, his shortcomings and limitations as president, his unfortunate business connections and scandals, and his final trials and tribulations, which redeemed him in the eyes of the public from his errors and the lax political morals of his administration, are sympathetically but realistically described by Martí in this Plutarchian biography.

There were other famous generals that attracted Martí's interest and whom he depicted with insight and imagination. All of them were heroes of the Civil War, and in later years figured more or less prominently in the political life of the country. When they died, Martí devoted a concise biographical sketch to each one. The most important were the following: T. A. Hendricks, vice-president under Cleveland, a mediocre politician, more ambitious than able, in Martí's estimate; Winfield S. Hancock, inexperienced in the political game, unsuccessful as a candidate of the Democrats in 1880, but prominent as a martial figure and a man endowed with excellent moral qualities; Philip Sheridan, of whose military exploits Martí wrote a vigorous synthesis; George McClellan, opposing candidate to Lincoln, culturally superior to most of his colleagues in arms, and equal to any of them because of his sterling character; John A. Logan, a picturesque orator, running mate of James G. Blaine in 1884 on the Republican ticket; and Benjamin Harrison, Republican presidential candidate elected in 1888.

Among the other political figures portrayed by Martí with great keenness and justice was Samuel J. Tilden, Democratic candidate in 1876, about whom Martí wrote several times with intense sympathy. The patriotic and self-sacrificing attitude with which Tilden accepted the unfair solution given by Congress and the Supreme Court to the indecisive election of that year, won the admiration of Martí and endeared Tilden to him. For this reason, his appraisal of that political contender is perhaps more generous than that of some American historians.

Martí did not live long enough to witness the end of the second administration of Grover Cleveland. Furthermore, in the year 1892, when Cleveland was elected for the second time, Martí stopped writing for the Spanish American press and devoted his entire energy to the task of organizing the Cuban Revolutionary Party and preparing the War of Independence. Had he been able to scrutinize Cleveland's second term as closely as he did the first, and had he written his conclusions, we may be sure that his judgment of Cleveland would have been very different from the one he left us. In his second administration, Cleveland became much more reactionary and imperialistic than he had revealed himself to be during his first term in the White House. Martí's rating of Cleveland is, therefore, far more laudatory than that of some historians.

Who, other than scholars, remembers today Judah P. Benjamin, Senator from Louisiana and later Attorney General and Secretary of State of the Confederation? Yet Benjamin was one of the most brilliant and cultivated minds of his time. After the Civil War he went to England and started life anew in London when he was already over sixty. Soon he became known as a writer of note and a pillar of British jurisprudence. When Benjamin died in 1884, Martí published a subtle and concise analysis of his life which has won the unique distinction of being available in English translation.[12]

Roscoe Conkling has already been mentioned. To him, as to so many other once famous orators, could be applied the following words written by Martí apropos of Wendell Phillips: "An orator shines for his speeches; but he remains only for what he does. If he does not sustain his words with his acts, his fame will evaporate even before he dies because he has been standing on a column of smoke."[13]

Conkling was probably the most eloquent and cultured of all political orators in the seventies and early eighties. He was a master of this art at the early age of twenty-five. He had the imagination, the fluency of words, the talent, the culture, even the handsome and dignified physical appearance that a truly great speaker should possess. But Conkling—like his worthy and inexorable rival within the party, James G. Blaine—used his intellectual powers and dexterity to serve his personal ambitions rather than the people. His extraordinary adroitness was always employed to enhance his political fortunes, to defend the interests of big business and the ruling class, or to crush his enemies, but never to uplift the humble or to improve their lot. He was aristocratic by temperament, arrogant, and contemptuous. In spirit and action, he was the exact antithesis of Wendell Phillips. While Phillips, notwithstanding his aristocratic lineage, cast his fate with the slaves and the workers, and devoted his life to their redemption, Conkling remained faithful to the conception of a plutocratic republic, governed by the wealthy. He had little or no use for the masses. As Martí says, his ambition was not to serve the people but to be served by them. With the ascension to power of Garfield and Blaine, Conkling was finally crushed by the latter. During the last five years of his life, he suffered, with stoic dignity, the humiliation of his defeat and the ingratitude and betrayal of his friends and colleagues within the party. In the misfortunes of his last years, he acquired a moral stature that his great triumphs never gave him. Martí expressed this idea in words that read as a perfect epitaph for Conkling: "He achieved glory in his defeat. He began to be great when he ceased to be ambitious." [14]

Given the ethical gulf that separated Martí from Conkling, we can hardly expect him to have written a panegyric when Conkling died in 1888. Yet the interpretative essay does complete justice to its subject. In the very opening paragraph we find a mixture of admiration for Conkling's mental powers and his mastery of the art of handling and dominating men, as well as scorn for the selfish use that he made of his great gifts. Martí begins his splendid portrait with the following words: "It will be difficult to find a more patent demonstration of the sterility of selfish talent than that given by the magnificent orator who died yesterday—the imperial commissar of Grant, the systematic genius during the presidency of Garfield, the implacable enemy of Blaine, the most brilliant and cultured of all the orators of the United States: Roscoe Conkling." [15]

Martí shows in this study a profound knowledge of the idiosyncrasies of Conkling and of the political game in which he played such a paramount role. He demonstrates here his rare insight and acumen in judging men and discovering their innermost impulses and ambitions. In depicting Conkling, Martí deprecates his lack of generosity—his arrogance and contemptuous attitude towards the humble classes. At the same time, he could not but admire Conkling's superb eloquence, his talent and culture, and above all his personal honesty at a time when integrity was not fashionable in public life.

Interpreter of the Social Panorama

WE COME NOW to the most copious part of Martí's reporting on the United States. It comprises fourteen out of the seventeen volumes he wrote about this country. The other three deal with men of letters, political leaders, and great personalities of various kinds, as we have already seen. The compilers of Martí's works gave the title of *North American Men* to these three volumes and *North American Scenes* to the other fourteen. A more appropriate title for the latter would have been "The North American Panorama." It would have conveyed a more precise idea of the full coverage Martí gives to every aspect of North American life in his articles to *La Nación* of Buenos Aires and to *El Partido Liberal* of Mexico.

A significant feature of this marvelous reporting is the fact that most of it takes the form of letters addressed to the respective editors of the above-mentioned journals. It is a subtle manifestation of that intense humaneness that prevailed in everything that Martí did or wrote. He had to feel that he was communicating personally and directly with some concrete and congenial reader who would understand and share his thoughts, his worries, and his emotions. All his chronicles are imbued with his own spirit; all of them are permeated with that tender love of humanity that characterized his personality and his life. Every page that he wrote is saturated with that "milk of human kindness" so bountiful in him.

Martí never ceased to consider the United States as the greatest experiment in democratic government that mankind had witnessed. His admiration for the wisdom and civic virtues of the founders and great leaders of the past never faltered. To the end of his life, he believed that the country's political institutions were exemplary. But his initial admiration for the democratic experiment suffered a severe setback when he began to watch it in practice. One perceives in his writings a sense of disappointment creeping in little by little. As he observed the shameful use that a good many politicians were making of democracy, how the financial barons exploited it to their greedy advantage, and how miserably the masses of voters failed at the polls, some degree of disillusion was inevitable.[1]

The worst aspect of American political activity, and the one that Martí criticized most often and most severely, was the unholy alliance between big business and professional patriots and politicians. This pernicious influence of bankers, manufacturers, and industrialists in all branches of the government frequently converted American democracy into a mockery and a farce. Martí had utter contempt for both types: the avaricious briber or financier, and the despicable politician who would, for a price, betray the trust and the interest of the people who had elected him. Martí castigated both with the sternest words he ever employed.[2] He fully agreed with—and quoted—Doctor Johnson's epigram that patriotism is the last refuge of a scoundrel.

Another aspect of the political mores that he loathed was the lack of honesty, decency, and dignity during a presidential campaign. A good example of his expressed distaste for the crude spectacle follows. Although written in 1885, it has a rather sad actuality for every honest and enlightened observer of the present-day political scene. Said Martí:

"A presidential campaign in the United States is a coarse and nauseating affair. By May, even before the nomination of party candidates, the contest is on.

"Once the candidates are designated by the Conventions, all sense of dignity is totally forgotten.... Mud-slinging becomes rampant. Deliberate lies and exaggerations abound. Blows are exchanged below the belt; candidates knife each other in the back. Every kind of infamy is judged to be legitimate. Any blow is justified if it stuns the political enemy. The man who can devise and carry out a villainous scheme, boasts proudly of his ingenuity. Even prominent men consider themselves released from the slightest obligations imposed by honor. Behind every sentence, the pistol butts employed in the elections of yesteryear—and even occasionally today—can still be perceived. It is a brutal custom that will disappear with the passage of time. In those months it is useless to scan the papers proclaiming the most contradictory opinions. An honest observer does not know how to analyze a battle in which all participants campaign in bad faith, and feel justified in doing so. One newspaper denies openly what another openly affirms. Deliberately, each one suppresses any item that might speak well of the opposing candidate. They completely disregard, on those days, the pleasure of honoring...." [3]

To understand the scorn Martí felt for these unpleasant manifestations and the failures of democracy in this country, we must remember that he struggled for it all his life and, therefore, idealized it. To see democracy scoffed at and ridiculed by the very persons charged with the duty of defending it, was a painful experience for him. Moreover, the United States was the freest country in the world, and the one that for a century had been upheld as a shining example of democracy. Given his profound faith in this political system, it must have been very disquieting and even foreboding for him to see how poorly it was working here after a century of experimenting with it.

Another aspect of the United States that disturbed Martí was the materialistic character of its civilization and the lust for power evident in many of the economic and political leaders. We find in his writings many cogitations on this trait of American character which he considered detrimental to the future of its culture, and an omen that presaged no good for his Latin America.[4]

The immoderate preponderance in this country of materialism over spiritual and cultural values he described many times with no little anxiety. This proclivity if not arrested in time—he reflected—would give a Phoenician orientation to the civilization of the United States and would exhaust itself in an ephemeral effort to conquer wealth. Thus he pondered in 1885: "Which spirit will prevail in the North American civilization: the Puritanical one, which represents the most judicious and transcendental affirmation of human rights, or the Carthaginian one of conquest and sordid profits?"[5]

From what has been said and transcribed we should not draw the wrong conclusion that Martí condemned wealth or the pursuit of it. He was far too much of a realist to concur in such an absurdity. What he abhorred was the propensity in this country to elevate the conquest of material wealth to the dignity of a national ideal, to the detriment of other values. The following remarks, written in 1887, prove that he knew how important and necessary material prosperity is for the well-being and stability of a country. They also demonstrate his admiration for our economic success. Similar expressions of pleasure in our improved standards abound in his chronicles:

"After an exploring look along these streets, and around these ports and cities, one thinks involuntarily of seas and mountains. How quietly impressive! How serene and powerful! And this prodigious nation has come to life as a result of the union in good faith, of America and Work, in the house of Liberty. To possess it is to guarantee the stability of the republic. A poor nation will be continually in anguish and revolt. To raise living standards is to create defenders of personal liberty and independence, and enough public spirit for their defense." [6]

Equally numerous are his reproaches of the perennial pursuit of material success and the idealization of it that he detected in our milieu. He deplored the scant recognition granted here to men of culture who had no social significance. The exaltation of money-making and of the money-makers, he considered a malady and a serious deficiency in American culture which would eventually undermine and corrupt our society. [7]

The acute social conflicts that Martí witnessed during the fifteen years of his residence in New York, attracted his interest and became the subject of some of his most searching chronicles. His descriptions and analyses of the social ferment taking place within the proletariat some seventy years ago, constitute one of the most interesting aspects of his exegesis of this country. Some of these articles possess an enduring quality not only because of their intrinsic literary value, but also because of the insight with which Martí studied the problems and the ideas expressed in them. They are an excellent guide to discovering Martí's social ideology. In these chronicles he revealed himself as an indefatigable fighter for economic justice. He followed the struggle with keen interest, and at times with indignation.

He never failed to express his deep sympathies for the workers and to denounce the avarice of the corporations and the great injustices they perpetrated. In spirit, he was actually a fighter in the labor ranks.

What distressed him most was to see so much poverty amidst so much wealth concentrated in a small percentage of the population. He could not understand the callousness with which the big corporations exploited and abused the working class. Four years before he came to the United States, Peter Cooper, a millionaire himself, had said: "There is fast forming in this country an aristocracy of wealth—the worst form of aristocracy that can curse the prosperity of any country.... Such an aristocracy is without soul and without patriotism. Let us save our country from this, its most potent, and, as I hope, its last enemy." [8]

The arrogance and the impunity with which the corporations would transgress the law and perpetrate their injustices without even moral sanction, was interpreted by Martí as a sinister omen for the democratic institutions of the United States and for Latin America as well. The unbridled power of the potentates of banking, industry, and commerce, and the rampant impudence with which they would bribe executives and legislators and corrupt the political life were for him foreboding signs of a deep change in the fundamental character of the republic. He wrote in 1889: "What is apparent is that the nature of the North American government is gradually changing in its fundamental reality. Under the traditional labels of Republican and Democrat, with no innovation other than the contingent circumstances of place and character, the republic is becoming plutocratic and imperialistic." [9]

The average wages of the time fluctuated in most industries between fifty cents and one dollar for ten hours of labor. Yet a rapidly expanding and prosperous economy was producing fat returns for the investors and employers. Each day the tremendous influx of immigrants increased the ranks of the unemployed. The supply of labor was, therefore, much greater than the demand, and employers used this advantage to exploit the workers to the limit. Capital fought tooth and nail the timid attempts to organize labor unions. The police were ever ready to suppress strikes and to protect capitalists' use of strike-breakers. Martí condemned, time and again, the violent methods advocated by the anarchist leaders, with the same energy with which he condemned the sordid employers. Indicative of his position in the great battle between the rich employers and the needy workers are the following paragraphs:

"The strike is on, a strike of thousands of men, in New York and Brooklyn...

"In their negotiations with the employees, the coach companies refuse to deal with the representatives appointed by the workers' guild: the employees, in mass, abandon the stables, in demand, not of higher salary, nor seeking fewer hours, but because they are to be deprived of the right of association; the companies, which are nothing more than associations linked together in mutual defense against the workers, want each worker to stand alone, facing them with his two hands and his hunger, without organization or support. In this way the employer can lower wages with impunity; and with the butter that they remove from the bread in 3000 homes, they purchase another horse for their coach, another seal coat for their daughter who already has one, another black-nosed dog for their mistress!" [10]

Intimately allied with the problem of relations between capital and labor in that period, was the torrent of immigration already referred to. Not only did the hundreds of thousands of

European and Asiatic workers who arrived yearly in the United States create very serious social problems, but they also brought with them social, political, and economic philosophies foreign to the American milieu. Since the early nineteenth century, some of these theories had been gathering momentum in Europe, and had agitated that continent. Along with the millions of stepchildren that Europe dumped on these shores during the last three decades of the century, she exported socialism, communism, anarchism, nihilism, Marxism, and several other social creeds. With these doctrines came their fiery apostles and propagandists to preach and foment social unrest. The extreme poverty and misery that afflicted the working class at the time, plus the greed and cruelty of big capital, served as a fertile ground for the dissemination of the new ideas. The years 1880 to 1895 constitute a period of great social ferment which Martí observed and analysed with vision and discernment in a long series of articles which can still be read today with interest and profit.[11]

Only a few of the infinite number of subjects pertaining to American life that Martí discusses in his articles have been touched upon. It is not possible to give here even an index of those not alluded to, notwithstanding the fact that among them we could find some of the most illuminating essays he ever wrote. Examples of these are the two articles in which he analyzes the Catholic problem in the United States,[12] which should be available in English.

Martí commented several times on the country's educational system for which he had little respect. What was repugnant to him was the proclivity in both elementary and high schools to strangle the originality latent in most children, thereby developing a "herd spirit." He also criticized, in the following and other similar remarks, the meager cultural content of the curriculum at both levels:

"To read, to write, to count: that is all they think children need to know. But to what avail is reading if the children are not imbued with the love for it, with the conviction that it is pleasant and useful, and through the harmony and greatness of knowledge, with a sense of joy in the upward surge of the soul? To what avail is the knowledge of writing if the mind does not feed on ideas, nor is the taste for them encouraged?

"To count, yes, that they teach in abundance.

"When they have already taught them—youngsters five years of age!—to count from memory to 100, these children are still unable to read a syllable.

"From memory! Thus they crop the intellect, as they do the hair. Thus they stifle the individual in the child, instead of encouraging the movement and expression of originality that every creature bears within him. Thus they produce a repulsive and sterile uniformity, a kind of liveried intelligence." [13]

The inevitable sequel to such a deficient method and to the absence of cultural background, Martí contended, was the emergence in the United States of the one-track man, routinary and mechanized, skillful in just one trade, with only one goal in life—the conquest of material wealth—but devoid of intellectual interests outside of what pertains to his little field of specialization. If prolonged indefinitely, this system of education and this obsession about money, would convert the United States into a country of technical barbarians.[14]

The commemoration of certain historical events, like the first centennial of the Congress of Philadelphia, of Washington's election, or the inauguration of the monument to the Pilgrims, etc., afforded him the opportunity to demonstrate how profound his knowledge of United States history was. Of great literary value are his epic descriptions of the inauguration of the Statue of Liberty, the Brooklyn Bridge, the Charleston earthquake in 1886, Coney Island, Buffalo Bill and his circus, the founding of a town in Oklahoma, student life in our great colleges, the beaches in summer and the winter resorts in the mountains, and many other aspects of American life and society. He reported with sympathy and sometimes with delight on every imaginable aspect of the nation's way of living: how Christmas was celebrated, the Fourth of July, Thanksgiving, and Easter; theatres, operas, concerts, and art exhibitions; labor rallies, parades, political meetings, boxing matches, baseball and football games; high school and college commencements, summer vacations; important political, social, or cultural events; famous restaurants like Delmonico's in New York; the fashions in every season; the distinguished artists who visited New York; everything, from foreign policy to Easter eggs. Never in the history of Spanish American literature has a country been described so minutely and so beautifully by any writer. To read these narratives is like watching a kaleidoscopic panorama or movie. Thanks to Martí's writings, the Spanish American readers of the last years of the century knew more about the United States than about any of their sister republics.

David and Goliath

WE COME NOW to the two episodes in Martí's life in which his ideals and deeds came into conflict with the policy of the United States government. In both cases he thwarted the designs of the Department of State. In the first incident, he assumed the leadership of the Latin American republics and advocated a goal contrary to that propounded by the Department of State. In the second, he acted as leader of the Cuban Revolutionary Party. To understand the importance of both events, a flash-back will be necessary here.

Of all the public figures active in his times, none attracted Martí's interest so persistently as James G. Blaine, as has already been shown. No other contemporary is mentioned and discussed by Martí so many times in his writings. None did he fear and dislike so heartily; none worried him so much. In temperament and ideals, Blaine and Martí were the very antithesis of each other. Antithetic, too, were their respective policies as leaders of the two racial or cultural blocks in which the two Americas are divided. Eventually these two prominent men came into direct contact, and a clash was inevitable.

When Martí came to the United States, Blaine was already one of the two most conspicuous leaders of the Republican party. His influence in American politics was perhaps even greater than that of Roscoe Conkling. Like Conkling, he was a brilliant lawyer and a powerful orator. He spoke for big business and was its most ardent defender in Congress. He was the mouthpiece for imperialist interests in all the positions he occupied: Congressman, Speaker of the lower house, Senator, Secretary of State under Garfield, Republican presidential candidate in 1884, Secretary of State again under Harrison, and so on. As in the case of Conkling, Martí admired in Blaine his unusual talent, his brilliant oratory, his dexterity, and his sagacity. But he had only contempt for Blaine's want of scruples, for the laxity of his public morals, and for the unrestrained personal ambition to which he subordinated everything. Blaine was devoid of that honesty, generosity, and sincerity that Martí considered indispensable to make any man really great. Thus in one of his many descriptions of him, Martí says epigrammatically: "Blaine, versatile and unbridled, perspicacious and dreaded, never great... Blaine, purchasable, who true to his character, buys and sells in the market of men...."[1]

On another occasion he attempts to explain in the following words, the hold Blaine had on the masses of the Republican party:

"Blaine pursues his enemies pitilessly, with the same ruthless tactics that they employ against him. Even in the unruly locks of hair lying on his forehead, the implacable passion of Blaine's politics stands revealed. His unusual aggressive temperament dazzles and attracts his very enemies, in this land of struggle and aggression. His versatility, his catholicity, the natural power of his words, have a strong appeal for men who, in their majority, lack these qualities. Even in these defects of Blaine:— the skillful simony of his political influence; the unperturbed ease with which he confronts serious and proven charges leveled against him; his stubborn use of crafty arts against those who oppose him; his obvious lack of scruples or tact in committing or concealing public sins—it seems that the mass of people see their own image and absolve themselves of all guilt, and that they find in this triumphant political sinner the sanction for their own unbridled desire for success." [2]

Similar unflattering references were frequently made by Martí in his articles sent to *La Nación* of Buenos Aires for ten years, and Blaine must have been apprised of them, especially during the period 1888-1892 when he was Secretary of State in Harrison's administration. It was during this period that Blaine convoked the first two Pan American congresses or conferences that took place in Washington: one in 1889, in which what later became the Pan American Union, was organized; and the other, the International American Monetary Commission that met from January 7 to April 3, 1891, in which Martí played a paramount role. These remarks will be limited to the latter.

For a long time, the silver interests had been agitating in favor of the adoption of:

First. Bimetallism and the equalization of gold and silver, to be fixed by international agreement.

Secondly. The universal assimilation of monetary types both of gold and silver and their legal international circulation for all purposes.[3]

The two propositions transcribed constitute a brief of United States policy as well as of the purpose of the 1891 conference. Twice before, in 1878 and 1881, similar conferences had taken place in Paris. In both instances, Washington had tried to convince the European powers of the advantages of adopting bimetallism, but the efforts failed, chiefly because of the opposition of England and Germany. In his introductory speech to the American Monetary Commission, the American delegate, Lambert Tree, gave a frank explanation of Secretary Blaine's purpose in calling the conference. Tree said: "It is certain that America is largely interested in establishing a bimetallic standard on which gold and silver will circulate as money on equal terms." [4] Later he added:

"The delegates of the United States, therefore, venture to propose that this commission recommend that the countries represented here unite through their respective governments in inviting a monetary conference of all the powers of the world, to be held at London or Paris in 1893 or 1894, to consider the subject of bimetallism, and if possible to come to an agreement about it so that silver may be maintained on equal terms with gold as a circulating medium." [5]

In other words, the United States, as the largest silver producer in the world, would derive a tremendous profit by persuading all the other nations to adopt bimetallism; but it had failed twice before in the effort. Now it requested the support of the Latin American republics to carry the program into effect in a third attempt. The support of the silver producing countries, like Mexico and Peru, could be counted on, and perhaps with their help the other delegates could be persuaded.

José Martí was Consul General of Uruguay in New York at the time, and on December 23, 1890, he was appointed, by cable, Minister Plenipotentiary and Delegate of that country to the "Congreso Monetario de Washington." [6] Unfortunately his credentials did not arrive until after the conference had started. For this reason, his name does not appear on the roll call of the first meeting.[7]

Martí was widely known among the delegates, including those of the United States. He was probably the only one who was fluent in the four languages spoken by the delegates at the convention. Although he could not participate in the opening meeting, he soon became the leader of the delegates from the non-silver-producing countries. A quick glance at the detailed Index of the *Minutes* reveals that he was the most active delegate of the conference and the one who played the most decisive role. Martí was elected to all the important committees, among them the "Committee to study the propositions of the Honorable Delegates from the United States." This Committee was composed of the delegates from Argentina, Brazil, Chile, Colombia, and Uruguay. After studying the American motion, the Committee relegated to Martí the task of writing and delivering its report, both in Spanish and English, to the plenary assembly.

The report written by Martí is a model of diplomatic skill and sagacity. He was well aware of the pressure brought upon Blaine by the silver interests and the bankers; he also realized how profitable it would be for the United States, and particularly for the interests concerned, to adopt bimetallism on a world-wide basis. But the great majority of the Latin American countries—to say nothing of the European ones—lacked silver, and therefore had little if anything to gain from the proposed plan. He did not believe that the moment was opportune for the adoption of an international coin or coins; nor was he in favor of pressing the other countries of the world into an agreement on this matter. He was in favor of it, but in due time, and at the appropriate moment.

Martí succeeded in injecting into the report some of his own principles, and even in denouncing certain tendencies of the United States already evident to him in 1891. Thus he wrote into the report: "It is not the province of the American continent to disturb the world with new factors of rivalry and discord, nor to reestablish, with new methods and names, the imperial system through which republics come to corruption and death." [8]

Taking into account the fact that England was opposed to the plan, and remembering that England was the only country that helped Spanish America to achieve independence, and afterwards had contributed more than any other to the economic development of that continent, he wrote:

"It is not the province of the American continent to raise one world against another, nor to mass in haste elements of diverse nature; but to treat in honesty and peace, as it is nobly proposed by the Delegates of the United States, with those countries which, in the doubtful hour of our emancipation, sent us their soldiers, and in the turbulent epoch of our reconstruction keep their purse open to our needs." [9]

Referring to the greed of the silver and banking interests, and indirectly to the pugnacious manner in which the Department of State was attempting to make the world adopt bimetallism, Martí says:

"Moderation in its use would certainly in due time, benefit the producers more than excessive and artificial circulation. Silver has, perhaps, no other enemy than the untoward pretensions of those seemingly bent on throwing upon the world with an uncertain value—inasmuch as the value has to be decided in part by the production—a production vast and incalculable." [10]

And always the champion of the small and weak Latin American countries, he adds: "The hands of every nation must remain free for the untrammeled development of the country, in accordance with its distinctive nature and with its individual elements." [11]

The report must have been a bitter pill for Blaine to swallow. He still had presidential ambitions and counted heavily on the success of the conference to boost his political fortune. The report, nevertheless, was accepted unanimously and the bimetallism dreams had to be shelved for the time being.

It is astonishing to discover how seriously Martí had studied economics and how solid his knowledge of this subject was.[12] For years he had been the editor of two journals devoted principally to fostering commercial relations with Latin America. Consequently he had to familiarize himself with economic theories and often wrote with authority on these matters.[13] Martí's ideas on the problem of bimetallism were known, and the interests concerned became alarmed when it was revealed that Martí had been appointed Uruguayan delegate to the Monetary Commission. The American lawyer, Horace S. Rubens, who knew Martí intimately, describing this episode of his life, wrote:

"Secretary of State James G. Blaine, urged by banking interests, proposed that the Spanish-American countries should, as a clarifying move, adopt the silver standard. Perhaps few people realized then how enormously such an adoption would, a few years hence, have assisted the Republican Party.

"High officials scrutinized Martí when he took a vigorous stand against the silver standard. For his logical arguments, and his courage in expressing them, he was hailed by his adherents with fresh delight. But in other quarters it was felt the time had come to show the courageous young orator that he was becoming injudicious.

"Shrewdly enough the silver interests selected a Cuban living in Washington as their intermediary in this delicate business, having a premonition perhaps that Martí would show himself no meek adversary but a person who must be handled diplomatically.

"Martí received his Cuban visitor with the most sensitive courtesy. He listened with incomparable patience if not with conviction to arguments, especially those touching his own 'personal interests.' At a telling moment he interrupted to say that, apparently, he had been most stupid, but he could not see how the silver standard could affect his own personal affairs. His visitor, emboldened, began to speak plainly, as plainly as outright bribery. Martí, first summarizing his intention, kicked his visitor out of the room.

"The immediate result was to be expected. Martí went before the Pan American Monetary Congress and spoke so convincingly of the wrongs of the silver standard that it had to be given up, even by its most sanguine advocates. In view of this incident it is not surprising that Spanish-Americans claim him an outstanding glory of Pan America. Of course his reputation everywhere for practical courage was immediately enhanced." [14]

The second occasion on which Martí frustrated American policy pertained to Cuba. It took place four years later, in 1895. Ever since Thomas Jefferson, at the very beginning of the century, had advocated that the United States should acquire or control Cuba, no administration during the nineteenth century deviated from that objective. England had the same ambition, and since she was the biggest naval power of the time, her own covetous views about the destiny of Cuba, deterred the United States from any violent move to annex the Island. Several times during the century, the offer was made to purchase it from Spain, in spite of the fact that the Spanish crown had repeatedly informed the United States minister in Madrid that Cuba was not for sale.[15] Even after the Cuban patriots had fought a heroic ten-year war (1868-1878), during which several countries had granted belligerency to the revolutionary Cuban government, the United States continued to make propositions of purchase to Spain without the slightest regard or respect for the will of the Cuban people. This callous indifference to the patriotic feelings of a neighbour who had fought more heroically for independence than any other nation of the New World, was a painful disappointment, not only to the Cuban patriots, but to other Latin American countries as well. The United States never recognized either of the two great struggles for Cuban independence (1868-1878 and 1895-1898), or granted rights of belligerency to the revolutionary governments in either case. On the contrary. Officially, it hindered the purchasing of armaments and the organization and dispatching of expeditions from its shores to Cuba. In 1826, at the Congress of Panama, it had vetoed Bolívar's plans to liberate Cuba. When Mexico had a similar project years later, she had to reckon with United States opposition to the independence of Cuba and abandoned the idea.

North American policy in regard to Cuba during the century was one of "patient waiting," as Jefferson had counseled. The coveted territories should remain in weak hands until the opportune moment. Such was Jefferson's advice, and all the administrations that succeeded his, followed it, as far as Cuba was concerned.

Inside the United States, two conflicting points of view divided big business in regard to Cuba. The expansionist and imperialist elements wanted the acquisition or annexation of Cuba, not only because of her strategic position commanding the entrance to the Gulf of Mexico, but also because it offered great possibilities for economic investments and a market for the country's products. On the other hand, the protectionist group, the "landed aristocracy," particularly the sugar, tobacco, and fruit growers' interests, opposed the annexation of the Island because Cuban products would then enter the United States duty free and would compete adversely with agricultural production. There were other arguments employed by those opposing the incorporation of Cuba into the American political system: her diverse racial and linguistic elements, her different cultural and historical background, the lack of democratic experience in her people, and other considerations, but the decisive factors for defending or combating the acquisition of Cuba were, on the one hand, economic and military, and, on the other, purely economic. When the economy of the United States ceased to be predominantly agricultural, and industry, manufacturing, banking, and commerce gained the upper hand, the advocates of the annexation of Cuba won the battle over their opponents.

The idea that perhaps the Cubans themselves might have something to say in the matter did not occur to either group —or to the government. With the characteristic disregard for the rights of small countries shown by all imperialist powers throughout history, the United States assumed that the destiny of Cuba was the exclusive concern of the Spanish crown and the American government. Fate had placed the Island less than one hundred miles away, and its acquisition or annexation was only "a matter of time and circumstances." The will of the Cubans was never taken into consideration prior to 1898. The expanding economy of the United States needed that fertile territory which, at the same time, represented a valuable outpost or bastion for the naval defenses of the southern shores against any future enemy. That was all that mattered.

The scorn with which some leading elements in this country looked upon the Cuban people was plainly and frankly demonstrated in 1889, at the time when the Harrison administration was once more considering the possibility of purchasing Cuba. On March 16, 1889, *The Manufacturer* of Philadelphia, one of the most important Republican journals, and, in the opinion of the *New York Evening Post,* "the only professedly high-tariff organ in the country that is conducted with decent ability,"[16] published an editorial under the title "Do we want

Cuba?" which showed extreme contempt for the people of the Island. In it *The Manufacturer* displayed its ignorance, its scorn, and its bad faith. After discussing the advantages of purchasing or annexing Cuba, the editorial described the handicaps that the incorporation of Cuba into the American political system would present. Referring to the inhabitants of the Island, *The Manufacturer* expressed this gallant and altruistic judgment:

"[The inhabitants] are divided into three classes, Spaniards, native Cubans of Spanish descent, and negroes. The men of Spanish birth are probably less fitted than men of any other white race to become American citizens. They have ruled Cuba for centuries. They rule it now upon almost precisely the same methods that they have always employed, methods which combine bigotry with tyranny, and silly pride with fathomless corruption. The less we have of them the better. The native Cubans are not much more desirable. To the faults of the men of the parent race they add effeminacy and a distaste for exertion which amounts really to disease. They are helpless, idle, of defective morals, and unfitted by nature and experience for discharging the obligations of citizenship in a great and free republic. Their lack of manly force and of self-respect is demonstrated by the supineness with which they have so long submitted to Spanish oppression, and even their attempts at rebellion have been so pitifully ineffective that they have risen little above the dignity of farce. To clothe such men with the responsibilities of directing this government, and to give them the same measure of power that is wielded by the freemen of our Northern States, would be to summon them to the performance of functions for which they have not the smallest capacity."

A few days later, on March 21, the *New York Evening Post*

in another editorial commented on the ideas expressed by *The Manufacturer* and reproduced approvingly the transcribed paragraph. The reaction of José Martí to such biased ignorance was not slow in manifesting itself. On March 25, the *Post* published, under his name, a long article in which, with great dignity, he defended his compatriots from the gratuitous defamations inflicted upon them by both journals. With his characteristic courage and passion for justice, Martí denounced the animosity expressed by both journals, but even in this instance of grievous offense to the dignity of his countrymen, he found words of praise for the United States. He said in part:

"This is not the occasion to discuss the question of the annexation of Cuba. It is probable that no self-respecting Cuban would like to see his country annexed to a nation where the leaders of opinion share towards him the prejudices excusable only to vulgar jingoism or rampant ignorance. No honest Cuban will stoop to be received as a moral pest for the sake of the usefulness of his land in a community where his ability is denied, his morality insulted, and his character despised.... They admire this nation, the greatest ever built by liberty, but they dislike the evil conditions that, like worms in the heart, have begun in this mighty republic their work of destruction. They have made of the heroes of this country their own heroes, and look to the success of the American commonwealth as the crowning glory of mankind; but they cannot honestly believe that excessive individualism, reverence for wealth, and the protracted exultation of a terrible victory are preparing the United States to be the typical nation of liberty, where no opinion is to be based on greed, and no triumph or acquisition reached against charity and justice. We love the country of Lincoln as much as we fear the country of Cutting....

"It is not to be expected, for the honor of mankind, that

the nation that was rocked in freedom, and received for three centuries the best blood of liberty-loving men, will employ the power thus acquired in depriving a less fortunate neighbor of his liberty.

"It is, finally, said that 'our lack of manly force and of self-respect is demonstrated by the supineness with which we have so long submitted to Spanish oppression, and even our attempts at rebellion have been so pitifully ineffective that they have risen little above the dignity of farce.' Never was ignorance of history and character more pitifully displayed than in this wanton assertion. We need to recollect, in order to answer without bitterness, that more than one American bled by our side, in a war that another American was to call a farce. A farce! the war that has been by foreign observers compared to an epic, the upheaval of a whole country, the voluntary abandonment of wealth, the abolition of slavery in our first moment of freedom, the burning of our cities by our own hands, the erection of villages and factories in the wild forests, the dressing of our ladies of rank in the texture of the woods, the keeping at bay, in ten years of such a life, a powerful enemy, with a loss to him of 200,000 men, at the hands of a small army of patriots, with no help but nature! We had no Hessians and no Frenchmen, no Lafayette or Steuben, no monarchical rivals to help us; we had but one neighbor who confessedly 'stretched the limits of his power, and acted against the will of the people' to help the foes of those who were fighting for the same Chart of Liberties on which he built his independence." [17]

For many years Martí had scrutinized painstakingly the course of the Washington policy towards Cuba and its relations with Spain, and he was very much alarmed when the spokesman for the imperialist interests, James G. Blaine, was appointed secretary of state by President Harrison. He also watched our diplomatic contest with England, in which the British lion was beginning to retreat before growing American industrial and naval power. Martí realized that the hour of decision was approaching. His anxiety grew at the idea of a possible understanding between Madrid and Washington by means of which Cuba would be annexed. The only deterrent so far had been England's own ambitions—and naval power—but England was becoming more and more involved in remote areas of conflict and increasingly preoccupied with the rising might of imperial Germany.

Besides the expansionist interests in the United States, which clamoured for the possession of Cuba, Martí had to fight their allies in Cuba. There was in the Island a small but economically powerful group who, seduced by the prospect of a duty-free market for their products in the United States, wanted annexation.

A third group that worried Martí was the *autonomistas* who advocated local autonomy under the Spanish flag. This group was composed of many of the most prominent men of culture in Cuba, and although its program did not have roots in the masses, it was supported by a large number of professional people and members of the upper class.

The last four years of Martí's life were consecrated to the preparation of the revolution and the education of the Cuban masses for the war of independence. In this task he revealed his powers of persuasion and organization, as well as his practical genius. So well had he organized the revolution and so efficient and self-sacrificing had been his leadership, that when he gave the order for the uprising, early in 1895, the ultimate expulsion of Spain from the island was assured. He succeeded in imbuing the Cuban patriots with his own spirit of sacrifice.

He had the satisfaction of dying with the conviction that Cuba would be free.

Now the United States found itself confronted with a *fait accompli*—an uprising in Cuba of far greater proportions than that of the ten-year war, better organized and coordinated. A civilian government was administering the affairs of a large part of the country, and the whole island was aflame. The revolutionary government had efficient agents in New York, Washington, and other cities, who kept both Congress and the public well informed of the progress of the revolution. But above all, there were fifty thousand Cubans in arms who would not listen to appeals, counsel, or threats. They adopted Patrick Henry's famous pronouncement and would not lay down their arms until independence was achieved. The cherished dreams of annexing the island had to be abandoned. The wave of indignation produced in this country by the crimes that "Butcher Weyler" perpetrated in Cuba, forced the hand of Congress and President McKinley, and the Joint Resolution of April 19, 1898, was approved despite the efforts of many a senator who had not yet discarded the hope of annexation. The Teller Resolution, passed on that glorious day in American history, ordered the administration "to leave the government and control of the Island to its people." The ideal for which Martí had suffered and struggled all his life, was at last achieved, in spite of Spain, in spite of many skeptical or selfish Cubans, and despite the designs and ambitions of Wall Street expansionist forces.

Martí was an impoverished, frail, and sickly man longing for death. But justice was on his side, and he possessed the purity of soul, the genius, and the moral fortitude necessary to battle the giants. At the appropriate moment, the noble indignation and sense of justice and fairness always latent in the masses of the North American people came to the rescue of his dream of freedom for Cuba. Unfortunately, he did not live long enough to witness one of the most altruistic movements recorded in the history of the United States.

However, the imperialist forces, momentarily arrested in 1898 by the strength of public opinion, surreptitiously crept back, and in 1902 imposed the Platt Amendment upon Cuba, thereby obliterating the Teller Resolution. The Platt Amendment not only tarnished the spirit of that Revolution, but converted Cuba into an economic dependency of Wall Street and a political vassal of the Department of State. As Harold Underwood Faulkner says after describing the process of Cuba's economic domination by Wall Street:

"From all this it is evident that Cuban wealth has fallen under American control and that Cuban political life from 1898 until 1934, and to some extent thereafter, has been largely directed from Washington. The result has been the impoverishment, degradation, and exploitation of the Cuban people. 'Cuba,' said one historian, 'is no more independent than Long Island,' and the history of her subjection presents a gloomy record." [18]

The preceding account of José Martí's life and deeds has been limited to that phase of his activities which brought him into contact with the United States and, to a certain extent, incorporated him into its culture and history. A complete portrayal of the man and his intellectual achievements would require a large volume, but such was not the purpose of the present sketch. Here the aim has been to give a clear idea of the extent to which Martí fostered the culture of the United States and interpreted it and made it known to North America's Spanish-speaking neighbors. His contribution to the cause of inter-American cultural relations stands out as the most prolific, fruitful, and enduring ever rendered by anyone from either continent. As William Rex Crawford remarked: "Those who imagine that cultural relations date from 1938 may do well to thumb the pages of some seventeen volumes that Martí wrote about the men and doings of the United States." [19]

In the annals of cultural relations between the northern and southern parts of the Western Hemisphere, there is no greater link than José Martí. No other man from either the Anglo-Saxon or the Latin block has ever done so much to make the spiritual and intellectual values of the United States known throughout the Hispanic world. And yet José Martí is practically unknown to the North American people. In January, 1953, Latin America will commemorate the first centennial of his birth. This sketch of his contacts with and services to the culture of the United States will serve as a modest contribution in English to the commemoration of that solemnity. May it also serve to arouse in the reader an interest in one of the most admirable figures mankind has produced. He made known throughout Spanish America the culture of the United States, shared its way of life, and endeavored to enrich it and make it more beautiful, more noble, more worthy of the great men whom he extolled and revered.

NOTES

Historical Perspective

1. Harold Underwood Faulkner, *American Political and Social History* (New York: F. S. Crofts & Co., 1941), p. 513.

2. George F. Kennan, *American Diplomacy, 1900-1950* (Chicago: The University of Chicago Press, 1951), p. 17.

3. The only biography worthy of José Martí available in English is that of the Cuban professor, Jorge Mañach, *Martí, Apostle of Freedom,* translated by Coley Taylor (New York: The Devin-Adair Co., 1950). Another study worth consulting is the one written by Gonzalo de Quesada y Aróstegui, also a Cuban, under the title "José Martí" to be found in *The War in Cuba* (New York: Liberty Publishing Press, 1896).

Life of a Hero

1. José Martí, *Obras completas* (Havana: Editorial Trópico, 1941), XXXIII, 55. Most of the quotations from Martí's writings included in this study are taken from either of the two most complete editions of his works: *Obras completas,* Havana: Editorial Trópico, 1936-1947, 70 vols.; and *Obras completas,* Havana: Editorial Lex, 1946, 2 vols., 4225 pages. In order to save effort and space, references henceforth to either of the two editions will be indicated by the words "Trópico" or "Lex," the volume and the page.

2. The life of Martí was one of perpetual renunciation of worldly goods and material benefits. Thus in 1892 he resigned his post in New York as consul of Argentina, Uruguay, and Paraguay because he considered it incompatible with his duties as leader of the Cuban Revolutionary Party, which he had just founded. During the same year he also sacrificed his fame as a writer and relinquished his salary as a columnist in several of the most important newspapers of Latin America, like *La Nación* of Buenos Aires, *El Partido Liberal* of Mexico, etc., and stopped contributing to the *New York Sun* in order to consecrate all his energies to the liberation of Cuba. Before this, he had lost his beloved son and his wife, because the latter refused to share his idealism and spirit of sacrifice.

3. José Martí, *Versos sencillos* (New York: Louis Weiss & Co., 1891), p. 16.

4. Two of these journals, *La Edad de Oro* (1889), and *Patria* (1892), were founded and edited by Martí; of others like *La América* and *El Economista Americano,* he was literary editor only.

5. Dana's memory was somewhat confused. The exact period during which Martí contributed to the *Sun* was twelve years as indicated above—1880-1892.

6. The *New York Sun,* May 23, 1895, p. 6.

7. Horace S. Rubens, *Liberty. The Story of Cuba* (New York: Brewer, Warren & Putnam Inc., 1932), p. 30.

8. Willis Fletcher Johnson, *The History of Cuba* (New York: B. F. Buck and Co., Inc., 1920), IV, 9-10.

Man of Culture and Ideals

1. Federico de Onís, *Antología de la poesía española e hispano-americana* (Madrid: Publicaciones de la "Revista de Filología Española," 1934), p. 34.

2. William Rex Crawford, *A Century of Latin American Thought* (Cambridge, Mass.: Harvard University Press. 1944), pp. 230-231.

3. Lex, II, 1845.

4. Isaac Goldberg, *Studies in Spanish-American Literature* (New York: Brentano's, 1920), p. 52.

5. Abel Plenn, "Book Review," *New York Times,* July 2, 1950, p. 4.

Man of Destiny

1. The idea that great heroes or leaders are only an expression and an instrument of the social forces and needs, and are forged by them, was expounded by Martí on many occasions. Thus, writing on the great abolitionist, Wendell Phillips, in 1884, he said: "Los grandes hombres, aun aquéllos que lo son de veras porque cultívan la grandeza que hallan en sí y la emplean en beneficio ajeno, son meros vehículos de las grandes fuerzas." (Lex, I, 1084.)

2. Trópico, XXXII, 168.

3. Lex, I, 271.

The United States in the Eighties

1. Allan Nevins and Henry Steele Commager, *History of the United States* (New York: Pocket Books, Inc., 1951), p. 302.

Martí, Chronicler of Transformation

1. *The Fear of Freedom* (New York: Doubleday & Company, Inc., 1951), p. 72.

2. Lex, II, 1209.

3. Trópico, XVII, 25.

4. Cf. José Martí, *Cartas a Manuel A. Mercado* (Mexico: Ediciones de la Universidad Nacional Autónoma, 1946), p. 146.

5. Lex, I, 1292, 1294.

6. En las elecciones ¡qué comprar los votos o cambiarlos en las urnas, o rebajarlos en las listas, cuando era menester! En las asambleas menores de los Estados que eligen los diputados a la Convención que ha de designar el candidato del partido a la presidencia, ¡qué excluir, con anatema de traición, a los que se negaban a votar en el interés de los políticos de oficio!

. . . .

"Una tienda abierta, donde se mercadea por los rincones el honor, han venido a ser las convenciones, un tiempo gloriosas, en que los delegados del partido en cada Estado se reúnen cada cuatro años a elegir su candidato para el primer empleo de la Nación. Toda una delegación se compraba con unos cuantos millares de pesos, así como esta suerte de delegados para serlo, había comprado, siempre de mala manera, en la asamblea menor del Estado, el nombramiento en virtud del cual podían luego en la convención nacional vender su voto. Y dinero para estas compras de delegaciones oscilantes, jamás faltaba, por haber tanta enorme corporación, y tanto atrevido empresario, interesado en el triunfo del candidato que, en recompensa de estos anticipos, ha prometido estar a su servicio. Así, como de un templo profanado se retiraron de la última convención las gentes blancas del partido. (Trópico, XXXI, 24-26.)

A Plutarchian Portrayer

1. Here is an example of the lyric exaltation of President Garfield in which Martí endows him with the same virtues he himself possessed:

Vivir en estos tiempos y ser puro, ser elocuente, bravo y bello, y no haber sido mordido, torturado y triturado por pasiones; llevar la mente a la madurez que ha menester, y guardar el corazón en verdor sano; triunfar del hambre, de la vanidad propia, de la malquerencia que engendra la valía, y triunfar sin oscurecer la conciencia ni mercadear con el decoro; bracear, en suma, con el mar amargo, y dar miel de los labios generosos, y beber de aire y agua corrompidos, y quedar sano: ¡he ahí maravillas! ¡Cuánta agonía callada! ¡Cuánta batalla milagrosa! ¡Cuánta proeza de héroe! Resistir a la tierra es ya, hoy que se vive de tierra, sobradísima hazaña, y mayor, vencerla. (*Ibid.*, XXVIII, 146.)

2. Lex, I, 1054.

3. *Ibid.*, p. 1195.

4. R. H. Tawney, *Religion and the Rise of Capitalism* (New York: Harcourt, Brace and Co., Inc., 1950), p. 235.

5. In the history of the United States, Wendell Phillips symbolizes the moral conscience of Puritan New England better perhaps than any other reformer. Phillips is one of the country's truly great human and ethical forces, whose spiritual stature has not yet been duly recognized. At a time when he was condemned and vilified by the advocates and beneficiaries of the big

profits system, José Martí proclaimed him as one of the noblest men this country had produced.

6. Reiterating the concept expressed in note 17 above, Martí wrote of Beecher:

Nada es un hombre en sí, y lo que es, lo pone en él su pueblo. En vano concede la Naturaleza a algunos de sus hijos cualidades privilegiadas, porque serán polvo y azote si no se hacen carne de su pueblo, mientras que si van con él, y le sirven de brazo y de voz, por él se verán encumbrados, como las flores que lleva en su cima una montaña. Los hombres son productos, expresiones, reflejos: viven en lo que coinciden con su época, o en lo que se diferencian marcadamente de ella; lo que flota les empuja y pervade: no es aire sólo lo que les pesa sobre los hombros, sino pensamiento: éstas son las grandes bodas del hombre; ¡sus bodas con la patria!

¿Cómo, sin el fragor de los combates de su pueblo, sin sus antecedentes e instituciones, hubiera llegado a su singular eminencia Henry Ward Beecher, pensador inseguro, orador llano, teólogo flojo y voluble, pastor hombruno y olvidadizo, palabra helada en la iglesia? Nada importa que su secta fuera más liberal que sus rivales; porque los hombres, subidos ya a la libertad entera, no necesitan de una de sus gradas.

Pero Beecher, criado en la hermosura y albedrío del campo por padres en quienes se acumulaban por herencia los caracteres de su nación, creció, palpitó, culminó como ésta, y en su naturaleza robusta, nodriza de su palabra pujante y desordenada, se condensaron las cualidades de su pueblo, clamó su crimen, suplicó su miedo, retemblaron sus batallas y sus victorias. El pudo ser la maravilla: ¡un hombre libre que vive en una época grandiosa! (Lex, I, 1064.)

7. I have translated the last sentence only. Following is the complete description. Indignation and tenderness are mingled here with pity for the innocent victims and rebuke for a social and economic system that tolerated such wretchedness amidst so much showy luxury:

...allá en las calles húmedas donde hombres y mujeres se amasan y revuelven, sin aire y sin espacio...allá en los edificios tortuosos y lóbregos donde la gente de hez y de penuria vive en hediondas celdas, cargadas de aire pardo y pantanoso; allí, como los maizales jóvenes al paso de la langosta, mueren los niños pobres en centenas al paso del verano. Como los ogros a los niños de los cuentos, así el *cholera infantum* les chupa la vida: un boa no los dejará como el verano en New York deja a los niños pobres, como roídos, como mondados, como vaciados y enjutos. Sus ojitos parecen cavernas; sus cráneos, cabezas calvas de hombres viejos; sus manos, manojos de yerbas secas. Se arrastran como los gusanos: se exhalan en quejidos. ¡Y digo que éste es un crimen público, y que el deber de remediar la miseria innecesaria es un deber del Estado! (Trópico, XXIX, 188-189.)

8. *Ibid.*, XXXV, 184.
9. Lex, I, 1072.
10. *Ibid.*, pp. 1154-1155.
11. *Ibid.*, p. 1160.

12. As far as I have been able to ascertain, this is the only essay of Martí so far translated *in toto* into English. Translated by Louis Gruss, it appeared in *The Louisiana Historical Quarterly,* XXIII (Jan., 1940), 259-264.

13. Lex, I, 1078.

14. *Ibid.,* p. 1169.

15. *Ibid.,* p. 1162.

Interpreter of the Social Panorama

1. In his opinion the very nature of the republic was being transformed from a democracy to an oligarchy by the corrupting power of big business, as the following paragraph attests:

...en todos esos hechos, únicos que hoy de veras ocupan la atención, se ve como todo un sistema está sentado en el banquillo, el sistema de los bolsistas que estafan, de los empresarios que compran la legislación que les conviene, de los representantes que se alquilan, de los capataces de electores, que sobornan a éstos, o los defienden contra la ley, o los engañan; el sistema en que la magistratura, la representación nacional, la iglesia, la prensa misma, corrompidas por la codicia, habían llegado, en veinte y cinco años de consorcio, a crear en la democracia más libre del mundo la más injusta y desvergonzada de las oligarquías. (Trópico, XXXVI, 12.)

2. Cf. "El Secretario de Marina Whitney" (Lex), I, 1221-1224.

3. Trópico, XXXI, 12-13.

4. It is extremely interesting to compare Martí's reflections on this subject with those of another keen observer of American idiosyncrasy and mores, Alexis de Tocqueville. In one of many passages in which he commented upon the acquisitive obsession and the excessive love of money which he had observed in this country, Tocqueville wrote some fifty years prior to Martí:

"In America then every one finds facilities, unknown elsewhere, for making or increasing his fortune. The spirit of gain is always on the stretch, and the human mind, constantly diverted from the pleasures of imagination and the labours of the intellect, is there swayed by no impulse but the pursuit of wealth. Not only are manufacturing and commercial classes to be found in the United States, as they are in all other countries; but, what never occurred elsewhere, the whole community is simultaneously engaged in productive industry and commerce." (*Democracy in America,* tr. by Henry Reeves, Esq. [New York: A. S. Barnes & Co., 1863], II, 35-36.)

5. *Trópico,* XXXI, 133.

6. *Ibid.,* XXVII, 99-100.

7. en este pueblo revuelto, suntuoso y enorme, la vida no es más que la conquista de la fortuna: ésta es la enfermedad de su grandeza. La lleva sobre el hígado; se le ha entrado por todas las entrañas: lo está trastornando, afeando y deformando todo. Los que imiten a este pueblo grandioso, cuiden de no caer en ella. Sin razonable prosperidad, la vida, para el común de las gentes, es amarga; pero es un cáncer sin los goces del espíritu. (*Ibid.,* XXX, 77.)

8. Quoted from: Vernon Louis Parrington, *Main Currents in American Thought*, (New York: Harcourt, Brace and Co., Inc., 1930), III, 280.

9. Trópico, XXXVII, 56.

10. *Ibid.*, p. 70.

11. Among other essays on these problems see the following: "Las asociaciones de obreros"; "El problema industrial en Los Estados Unidos"; "La revolución del trabajo"; "Las huelgas en los Estados Unidos"; "Las grandes huelgas en los Estados Unidos"; "Grandes motines obreros"; "El proceso de los siete anarquistas de Chicago"; "Un drama terrible"; "La inmigración en los Estados Unidos" in Lex, I, 1545; 1644; 1672; 1677; 1681; 1699; 1736; 1842; 2042, respectively.

12. Cf. "El cisma de los Católicos en Nueva York: and "La excomunión del padre Mc Glyn," *Ibid.*, pp. 1781 and 1819, respectively.

13. Trópico, XXXIII, 110.

14. El hombre máquina rutinaria, habilísimo en el ramo a que se consagra, cerrado por completo fuera de él a todo conocimiento, comercio y simpatía con lo humano. Ese es el resultado directo de una instrucción elemental y exclusivamente práctica. Como que no hay alma suficiente en este pueblo gigantesco: y sin esa juntura maravillosa, todo se viene en los pueblos, con gran catástrofe, a tierra....

De leer, escribir y contar no se pasa en la escuela pública. Y de la escuela pública, a la faena, al espectáculo de lujo, al deseo de poseerlo, a la vanidad de ostentarlo, a las angustias crueles e innobles de rivalizar con el del vecino. (Trópico, XXXII, 68-69.)

DAVID AND GOLIATH

1. I have translated only two sentences of the following scornful description of Blaine. Rarely did Martí use such strong language; but Blaine epitomized for him all the greed, all the injustice, and corruption of the big profits system, so aptly defended and symbolized by the 1884 Republican candidate. It was apropos of that very Republican convention in which Blaine was nominated that Martí wrote this vigorous denunciation of him:

Blaine, que con el rufián habla en su jerga, y con el irlandés contra Inglaterra, y con el inglés contra Irlanda, y fué el que quiso sujetar en hipoteca al Perú, bajo la garantía y poder americanos al pago del reclamo de un aventurero, con quien andaba en tomares y decires y por cuyos intereses velaba con tal celo que convirtió al Ministro de los Estados Unidos, muerto después del bochorno, en agente privado del reclamo, que abusaba del gran nombre de su pueblo para que los beligerantes reconociesen la impura obligación; Blaine, móvil e indómito, perspicacísimo y temible, nunca grande; Blaine, acusado con pruebas, y con su propia confesión escrita, de haber empleado espontánea e intencionalmente, en anticipo de una recompensa en acciones, su autoridad como Presidente de la Casa de Representantes para que se votara una ley que favorecía indebidamente los intereses de un ferrocarril en que ya tenía, por servicio no menos criminal, una buena parte;—Blaine, que no hablaba de poner orden en su casa, sino de entrarse por las ajenas, a buscar, so pretexto de tratados de comercio y paz, los caudales de que los errores económicos del partido republicano han comenzado a privar a la nación;—Blaine, mercadeable, que a semejanza de sí propio,—en el mercado de hombres compra y vende. Tal convención eligió a tal candidato. Blaine fué el electo. Por debajo de las banderas alquiladas, y de entre los delegados vendidos que habían ayudado al triunfo, salieron, llenos de rubor y de ira, los que con una generosa esperanza habían acudido a la Convención para ver de nombrar a un hombre honrado. (*Ibid.*, XXXI, 36-37.)

2. *Ibid.*, XXXIII, 120.

3. *Minutes of the International American Monetary Commission*, January 7 —April 3, 1891. Called by James G. Blaine, Secretary of State of the United States. Washington, D. C., 1891.

4. *Ibid.*, p. 31.

5. *Ibid.*, p. 35.

6. *La Republica del Uruguay y el Prócer Cubano José Martí* (Montevideo: Ministerio de Relaciones Exteriores, 1917), p. 1.

7. The official "Minutes" give no explanation for the absence of his name from the list of delegates attending the first meeting. But since the formal credentials were not sent until January 15, 1891, presumably he was not considered an official delegate until the accrediting document arrived.

8. *Minutes of the International American Monetary Commission*, p. 44.

9. *Loc. cit.*

10. *Ibid.*, p. 47.

11. *Ibid.*, p. 48.

12. He wrote on these problems many times. One of his best economic essays is his own commentary on the Monetary Commission, entitled "La conferencia monetaria de las repúblicas de América." (Lex, II, 259.)

13. For an appraisal of Martí's economic ideas, see my *Fuentes para el estudio de José Martí* (La Habana: Ministerio de Educación, 1950), p. 399.

14. *Op. cit.*, pp. 28-29.

15. The history of the shoddy relations with Cuba has never been written in English. The most exhaustive study on the subject is Herminio Portell Vilá's *Historia de Cuba en sus relaciones con los Estados Unidos y España* (La Habana: Jesús Montero, Editor, 1938-1941), 4 vols. It is not available in English yet, and its translation is already overdue. Another more succinct but valuable source of information is *La expansión territorial de los Estados Unidos a expensas de España y de los países hispano-americanos* by Ramiro Guerra y Sánchez. (La Habana, Cultural, S.A., 1935.)

16. "A protectionist view of Cuban annexation," *The New York Evening Post*, March 21, 1889, p. 4.

17. José Martí, "A Vindication of Cuba," *The New York Evening Post*, March 25, 1889, p. 9.

18. Harold Underwood Faulkner, *op. cit.*, p. 528.

19. William Rex Crawford, *op. cit.*, p. 230.

www.ingramcontent.com/pod-product-compliance
Lightning Source LLC
Chambersburg PA
CBHW031714230426
43668CB00006B/209